Confessions of an Ex-Feminist

LORRAINE V. MURRAY

CONFESSIONS OF AN EX-FEMINIST

IGNATIUS PRESS   SAN FRANCISCO

Cover photograph © Peter Brutsch

Cover design by Riz Boncan Marsella

Copyright © 2008 by Lorraine V. Murray
All rights reserved
ISBN 978-1-58617-225-1
Library of Congress Control Number 2007928634
Printed in the United States of America ∞

To Monsignor Richard Lopez,
who led me, ever so gently, to the light

"Why should not I love thee,
Jesu, so much in love with me?"

—Gerard Manley Hopkins
"O Deus, ego amo te"

CONTENTS

ACKNOWLEDGMENTS

This book is a dream that has been taking shape in my head for years, and it would not have come to fruition without encouragement from many people. I am deeply grateful to my husband, Jef, who provides our household with delectable meals and homemade wine and helps banish the demons of doubt that often assail me. He read an early draft of this book, made suggestions, and encouraged me to complete it. I also thank the people who frequently express enthusiasm about my writing projects: my mother-in-law, Lou Craig; my sister, Rosemary Mende; my cousin, Julie Anderson; my aunt, Rita Pope; my childhood buddy, Alice Aznar; and my colleagues at the Pitts Theology Library, especially M. Patrick Graham, John Weaver, and Fesseha Nega. Two other people took an early look at the manuscript and encouraged me: Monsignor Richard Lopez, who is my spiritual director, and Joseph Pearce, a friend, who is the editor of the *St. Austin Review*. Joseph was kind enough to shepherd the book to Ignatius Press, where the editors have added the finishing touches. My nephew, Rick Mende, and my nieces, Jennifer Metcalf and Christina Edgar, are always cheering me on, and I thank God for their presence in my life. And for all the lunches, conversations, hugs, and encouragement, a big thank-you to my best friend, Pam Mottram!

Please note that some names in the text have been changed in order to protect individuals' privacy.

INTRODUCTION

Warning: This is a dangerous book. It may make some feminists see red, and some atheists think black thoughts. It may rile up readers who think all religions are equally valid and cause consternation in the hearts of some Catholics, who think they can pick and choose among the dogmas of their faith.

It is a book that had to be written, although I will admit that I resisted the impulse for a long while. Whenever I would think, "I must tell the tale of my conversion experience", I would realize that this entailed divulging what came before, which included the years when I waged a vendetta against Catholicism. But it also meant describing my childhood as a Catholic schoolgirl, when one of my biggest problems was grappling with what were called "impure thoughts".

I wondered if it was presumptuous to believe that the details of my life were special enough to record for others to read. But just as I was thinking along these lines, a student would come by my desk at the theology library where I work, and we would somehow broach the topic of conversion. And if I were to mention my return to Catholicism after more than twenty years away, a predictable thing would happen.

"What made you come back?" the student would ask. And I would fumble around, because the question is so much like asking a person who has been married twenty-five years, "What made you fall in love?" How could I explain, in a matter of a few minutes, how and why I had come back to the religion that I had so thoroughly and passionately despised for so many years?

This dilemma sent me to my computer to try to hammer out a few lines about my return to Catholicism. And, sure enough, as I tried to explain why I came back, I had to tell why I had left, which meant telling how I arrived there in the first place. There was just no getting around it: I was going to have to tell the whole tale.

Now, if you are fortunate enough to have led a sunny life with myriad memories of joyful picnics and sweet meanderings along the seashore, writing your life story might be a happy endeavor to undertake. For me, though, the project has meant reliving bitter moments, such as a childhood crippled by my father's gambling addiction, and my thoroughly wild years in college, when I lived in an apartment complex aptly nicknamed "Sin City".

Some readers, I fear, may be scandalized by this book, when they realize how many years I went my merry way as a sinner, dabbling in sex, drugs, and rock and roll, and launching my own personal war against God. Other readers may glimpse themselves in these pages and think, "Oh, dear, I have been through *that*, just as she has! This all sounds familiar, and I thought I was the only one!"

The belief that I was the only one plagued me for years. There were times when I suspected that other people had gone to college to write term papers, study for exams, graduate, and get married, all the while obeying social conventions, saying their prayers, and paying their bills.

Then there was me. It is true that I went to college to get a series of degrees, but I did so by partying like a fiend and touting the virtues of nihilism. The T-shirt for my life would have echoed the words of Dostoyevsky: "If God is dead, then anything is possible." Of course, college days often are connected with rebellion, but my style of rebellion lasted over twenty years, and as a philosophy teacher, I was able to tempt others to join me.

I hope this book finds its way into the hands of others who were, or are, as nihilistic as I was, so they will know they are not alone and may realize that, no matter how deep the hole they have dug, there is always an escape route.

C. S. Lewis once warned that an atheist could not be too careful about what he reads, because Bibles are left open all over the place, and unbelievers would have to guard themselves against the danger of taking a glimpse.[1] I hope that many people, atheists as well as believers, will take more than a glimpse at this book and know that they were sufficiently warned.

I

Fall from Grace

When my mother showed up in labor at Saint Joseph's Hospital, the sisters urged her to keep her legs crossed. They were afraid she would have the baby before the doctor arrived. Although Dr. Ralph Bellantoni's name appears in my baby book as the one officially presiding over the event, my mother always suspected that the Sisters of Charity had delivered me.

I made my entrance into the world at 8:30 P.M. on August 29, 1947, which was the day commemorating the beheading of poor Saint John the Baptist. Born in Yonkers, I went home to a humble townhouse in Elmhurst, with a housewife named Grace and a taxi-cab driver, Gaspar Viscardi, known as Tom.

I recall little of the very early years of my life. There are teeny images and whispers here and there in my memory bank but no coherent thread of events. One mental snapshot has me standing outside in the yard behind our two-story house, playing with my sister, Rosemary. When we were thirsty, we called upstairs to my mother, and she would tie a string around a plastic cup of water and slowly send it down to us. We were in the yard playing without adult supervision, but this was typical of the time: Adults figured that if there were no screams of anger or agony, the children were safe.

At our Elmhurst townhouse, located at 5754 Eightieth Street, my mother would sometimes place me in a playpen on the front lawn, where she could watch me from the window while doing housework. According to an oft-told family legend, people walking by would stop to admire the sweet, chubby-cheeked baby. It was at that point that I grabbed the bars of my playpen, shot them a stern look, and uttered one of my favorite first words: "DOPE!"

I have little doubt that I learned that word from my sister, who was two years older than I. Family lore has it that when my mother brought me home from the hospital, wrapped in a cotton blanket, she bent down to show the new baby to Rosemary, and a tiny hand dangled from the blanket at a tempting angle before my sister's face. She took a nip, I screamed, and thus was born a contentious relationship that lasted throughout our childhood.

Over the years, I probably heard the same thing a thousand times. As my sister and I would be thrashing each other for some suspected grievance, or measuring the exact dimensions of a piece of cake we were expected to split, my mother would gesture toward heaven and say, "They told me to have two! They said if I had two, they would play together!" I am not sure to whom "they" referred, but I suspect it was her aunts. In any event, the implications of her words were fairly obvious: She hoped to shame her children into getting along better with each other, but it never worked.

I grew up with a certain odd gratitude for the fact that my mother had gone ahead and "had two". She often mentioned the harrowing circumstances of my sister's birth, and although she supplied no details, she told us darkly that she had "nearly died", and the doctors had warned her against having more children. Her words became deeply imbedded in my memory, and when I was finally old enough to give birth myself, the prospect filled me with dread.

Generally, when I think about my childhood, the color I come up with is a dull gray. I remember sparring with my sister; being chased around the house by my father, his belt in hand; and listening to my mother screaming at us to behave. I have little trouble believing in the biblical story about the Garden of Eden, because I think each of us, in our own lives, relives the original conflict, some in early years and some later. When I have tried to pinpoint the exact source of my unhappiness, I draw a blank, but I suspect it had to do with my father gambling, my mother fretting over money, and the family's fall from grace, when my mother had to go back to work.

My mother, Grace Mary Bibbo, had grown up in East Harlem in a brownstone at 428 East 120th Street, with three brothers and two sisters. Her mother, Rose Mary, was the daughter of Joseph and Josephine Andriuolo, immigrants from Piaggina, Italy. Her father, Antonio Bibbo, was a plasterer who believed so strongly in education that he managed to produce, among his six children, a doctor, two teachers, and a nurse.

I was a grown woman before I learned that my maternal grandfather was fiercely anti-Catholic. The story my aunt told went like this: As a little boy in Basilicata, Italy, Antonio Bibbo decided to climb a tree and peer into the courtyard of the rectory, where he spied the village priest cavorting with a woman. Evidently that scene was enough for him, as he gave up on Catholicism entirely and later joined the Masons. His bitterness ran so deep that, after he married, he tried to prevent his wife and children from going to Mass. Still, despite his efforts, his three daughters received the sacraments at nearby Holy Rosary Church, married Catholic men, and raised their children in the faith.

My maternal grandmother, Rose, was a typical, self-sacrificing Italian mother, who spent her days preparing elaborate meals for her husband and six children, which often included cutting out pasta noodles by hand and hanging them to dry on the backs of the dining room chairs. The family photos show a very plump woman with a sweet, shy expression, but she must have wielded a subtle power over her husband, because after they would have a particularly ferocious disagreement, he would throw his hat into the house before entering. If the hat was not tossed back, he knew it was safe to enter.

My mother was the oldest daughter of their three girls, and after high school, she enrolled at Hunter College, where she majored in French. She was teaching school when she met Tom Viscardi, a rather dashing man of Sicilian ancestry, at a party. He was the son of Francesco and Rosina Viscardi and had grown up in Greenwich Village during the days when it was an Italian enclave. He was evidently quite attracted to the witty and voluptuous schoolteacher named Gracie and wrote her tender love letters and brought her flowers. They had much in common: their Italian heritage, their Catholic background, and even their Latin good looks. But there was a big difference that would come back to haunt them: He had dropped out of school in sixth grade to help support his mother, brother, and two sisters after his father's death.

They married when they were twenty-nine, and I'm sure they expected marriage to be a kind of paradise and didn't realize they would encounter some vipers there. Maybe my parents didn't think the disparity in their backgrounds would matter, but my father's difficulty getting jobs, coupled with his love of gambling, soon put a strain on their relationship. My mother had quit her teaching job after marrying my father and was still a full-time housewife when, at age thirty-three, she gave birth to my sister. But then, two years later, when, despite her doctor's warnings, I made my appearance in the world, financial problems reared their ugly heads, and she very reluctantly hung up her apron and headed back into the classroom.

Today, her combination of motherhood and career might seem commonplace, but in the 1950s, it was extremely rare. It would be tempting to tag her as an early feminist, but that would be far from the truth. She often told her daughters about her unfulfilled dream, which was simply to do what other mothers of the time were doing: tending to their children and keeping house full-time. "I always wanted to stay home with you girls" was the mantra she repeated longingly during our childhood.

A heart-wrenching story she repeated often had her waiting for the bus one morning and hearing her babies wailing at home. She cringed when someone in the crowd commented darkly on mothers who didn't take proper care of their little ones.

I am fairly certain that she thought her return to teaching would be a stop-gap measure until family finances improved, but it seems that my father's earnings too often vanished at the racetrack. The result was that my mother ended up teaching for over twenty-five years. The repercussions of their money problems were long-lasting: My sister and I were left in the care of various babysitters, whom we abhorred, and my mother felt guilty about abandoning us.

These were the days before anyone had heard of gambling addictions, and most of the men in the family placed bets on horses as a matter of routine. For some men, that wasn't a problem, but for others, like my father, the lure of striking it rich was irresistible, and they didn't seem able to withstand the temptations at the racetrack. When I was in my twenties, I went with my father to the track one day, and it took only one race for me to understand the thrill.

As the horses thundered around the track, I had the sense that time was standing still and that nothing in the world mattered except which horse would eventually be declared the winner. As they neared the finish line, every worry, every anxiety, and every sour memory was washed away from my consciousness, because all I cared about was whether or not I might be a winner that day. On the days when my father did win, he was eager to continue betting to try to double or triple his winnings. If he did not win, he wanted to return another day to make up for his losses.

In the early photos in the family albums, the look on the two little girls' faces is often sullen. I wonder if the feelings of discontent that arose from my mother's unsatisfied longing to stay home and my father's unfulfilled dream of striking it rich didn't permeate our lives like a virus. Very young children live in the present moment, and when their mother leaves them, they do not realize she will return in the future. And so, each morning, when my mother walked out the door, leaving us in the care of the dreaded babysitters, my sister and I pitched a huge and dramatic fit.

❦

I don't know if my mother was actually correct about the sisters delivering me, but I do know that the ladies in their long black dresses, with their starched white wimples and black Rosary beads clicking rhythmically as they walked, played a substantial role in my childhood understanding of what God expected of me.

Sister Lawrence Therese, my first-grade teacher at Ascension Catholic School in Elmhurst, explained that the soul was white, and when she sketched it on the blackboard, it was always circular. For many years, the soul was as real to me as the heart that I felt beating in my chest, and it was somehow connected with the snowy wimples that the nuns wore. As for sin, I pictured it as a black slash upon the pristine white circle.

At home, my own sins consisted of endlessly arguing with my sister and thoughtlessly walking away from Monopoly games when she was winning. At school, because I was very chubby, I was often the brunt of sinfully cruel teasing from my classmates, so I learned early what it feels like to be a misfit. The class photos show a tense-looking, plump, dark-skinned girl with a head of frizzy curls, the result of experimentation by her older cousins who were attending beauty school.

I decided early on that since I wasn't going to be one of the pretty, popular girls, I would excel at schoolwork. My parents were the type who didn't make too big a deal out of a report card with all As but would express great consternation if a single B showed up. I feared their disapproval more than anything else, so I worked tirelessly to learn my lessons.

"Why did God make you?" was one of the first questions in the *Baltimore Catechism*, one of the school books that I carefully protected with a home-fashioned cover made from a brown grocery bag. "To know him, to love him, and to serve him in this world and to be happy with him forever in the next" was the reply I proudly memorized, although it would be years before the notion of loving and serving God would make any real sense to me.

2

Bless Me, Father

"Jesus Christ!" my mother screamed, as she chased us through the house—and she wasn't praying. Her nerves were thoroughly frazzled by the time she arrived home from teaching. She still had papers to grade and lesson plans to fill out for the next day, and she also had to cook supper, wipe our runny little noses, bathe us, and get us into bed.

Of course, we weren't aware of her many burdens, so we acted like typical kids. We accidentally knocked over glasses of milk at supper, spread cookie crumbs in the living room, and noisily resisted the evening plunge into a soapy tub of warm water. A perfectionist at heart, my mother wanted a spotless, tidy house and children who didn't have to be told four times to put on their pajamas, but we wreaked havoc with her best-laid plans.

One day, she'd had enough of our shenanigans: She packed a bag, climbed into the car, and bid us goodbye. We were frantic with worry, but she merely drove around the block a few times and then returned a short while later. I never forgot that day, however, because the one thing in life that I feared, more than anything else, was losing my mother.

I worshipped my pretty, dark-eyed mother and would trail her around the house, asking her, over and over, "Do you love me?" It was a childish game on some level but also deadly serious, because I yearned for the assurance of her love. Exasperated, she would switch off the vacuum cleaner and say that of course she loved me. Thrilled by the attention, I probably drove her to the brink of madness by switching to a new litany: "You are the most beautiful woman in the world."

One day my mother told me that I had once lived inside her belly, a fact that impressed me deeply. No wonder I felt so close to her and loved her to distraction! Unfortunately, because I had no inkling about the male's role in reproduction, I concluded that my father was not even related to me, and I regarded him rather coldly as a man who just happened to be married to my mother.

In my toddler days, I can recall that he sat me on his lap and read me the funny papers, but once I began school, he seemed to recede into the background, entering the children's sphere only to dole out punishment. In the style of Sicilian fathers, he would remove his belt and chase Rosemary and me around the house when we had done something wrong. I don't recall that he actually made a direct hit, but I do know that he bought us comic books later as a peace offering.

For better or worse, my image of God the Father was modeled after my own dad: distant, noncommittal, undemonstrative, and somewhat scary when angered. Maybe because I felt so close to my mother and went first to her with my complaints and questions, I fully embraced the Church's depiction of the Blessed Virgin Mary as an intercessor. Surely Mary would take my pleas to Jesus, just as she had brought him the request of the bride and groom at the wedding feast at Cana.

The communion of saints was another Catholic doctrine that was echoed in my family experiences. We were taught that there was a vast spiritual family that connected the pilgrims on earth, the saints in heaven, and the souls in Purgatory,

who would one day be in heaven. Although I had only one
sister, this interconnectedness made perfect sense to me, since
I grew up feeling that I was part of a huge crowd.

My "communion of saints" included six female and four
male cousins, plus a generous assortment of aunts and uncles.
Thanksgiving Day brought my mother's side of the family
to Aunt Lillian and Uncle Savy's one-bedroom apartment
on East Mosholu Parkway in the Bronx, where nine adults
and seven children somehow managed to fit. While the adults
sipped cocktails, the older cousins acted in a less-than-
saintly fashion by chasing the smaller kids around, bran-
dishing Aunt Lily's fur coat, which had scary fox heads,
complete with beady eyes.

When I was three months shy of my seventh birthday, on
May 29, 1954, I received my First Holy Communion. Sister explained that we would be receiving Jesus Christ, body
and blood, soul and divinity, in the Communion Host. We
were not simply attending a memorial service, she said, in
honor of someone like George Washington, who had died
long ago. Instead, during Mass, the living God became
present in a real way on the altar. This was a miracle, Sister
explained, just like Christ rising from the dead.

I heartily embraced the miracle that was called the Real
Presence. Maybe I couldn't understand the finer points of
theology, but I trusted that I would be receiving Jesus, which
would make the day immeasurably special. Like the other
little girls, I was also thrilled on a much more down-home
level: We would get to dress up in beautiful, Communion-
wafer-white dresses, complete with frothy veils and pristine
patent-leather shoes.

The sacraments brought hidden graces into our lives, Sister explained. Even if we didn't feel different after receiving Communion, God's grace was still pouring into our souls and helping us to become better people. God could be trusted to give us grace even on the days when we ourselves might feel that nothing was happening. Sister also reminded us, with a stern look at her grubby little charges, that human beings will never be perfect. And when we failed, as we surely would, Jesus had provided another sacrament, which was called confession, to restore us to grace.

Every Saturday, Rosemary and I went to confession, where we admitted our failures aloud. We knew that the priest stood in for Jesus in the confessional and that we were really confessing to God. "Bless me, Father, for I have sinned", I said, as I knelt in the booth, with a screen between me and the priest that kept my identity hidden.

A scrupulous child, I decided it would be better to err on the side of mentioning too many instances of my sins than too few, so I settled on the magic number of one hundred. I'm sure the priests must have choked back a chuckle when they heard a little girl saying, each week, that she had fought with her sister "one hundred times" and disobeyed her parents "one hundred times".

When it came to my sister, perhaps that number wasn't too farfetched. Despite the fact that every week I promised God that I would amend my life, I couldn't seem to stop squabbling with Rosemary. I was the ultimate tattler, a nightmarish little sister who teased her big sister mercilessly. When she reached her boiling point, she would take out her vengeance on my beloved stuffed dog, Poppa Pluto. When Rosemary threatened to string him up from the ceiling, I wept profusely, since I thought he was alive, and I could easily imagine his fear. His tattered body still bears the scars of our many fights as well as my desperate attempts to comfort him.

In many ways, that battered dog became an emblem of love and redemption in my childhood. After his eyes had been ripped off in a battle, my mother lovingly embroidered him new ones. She also stitched his head back on and repaired his paws. If I had trouble as a child understanding the notion that Christ had suffered on the Cross for my sins, I certainly understood the pain that Poppa Pluto was undergoing because of my own inability to get along with my sister.

My parents were strict disciples of the school of economics that promised you could become rich by buying and selling real estate. Their adherence to this dogma led to the first of many upheavals in our lives, when they moved the family to a home in Bayside, New York, where I began third grade at Saint Robert Bellarmine School. Before long, though, the for-sale sign showed up again, and we were saying a sad good-bye to all the aunts, uncles, and cousins and moving once more, this time to Miami.

During my elementary school years, the family moved more than six times, and for a child who was shy and melancholy by nature, the disruptions were agonizing. I began to long for what I thought of as an ordinary life, which apparently I would never have. It would consist of a father who made a good living, a mother who stayed home, and a feeling of belonging somewhere in a permanent sense. One of my aunts, who lived in the same house for over forty years, laughingly referred to my parents as gypsies at heart, and her appraisal seemed right on the money.

To explain why we were leaving New York, my parents said they were tired of the harsh Northern winters. Years later, though, this same aunt told me that they hoped to make a clean start in Florida. It seems that my dad was still involved heavily in gambling, and my mother believed the move would separate him from unsavory friends and tempting situations in New York. Her dream was to become a full-time homemaker in Miami, while my dad became the provider.

That dream, however, did not materialize, because not long after we moved to Miami, she began teaching at Highland Park Elementary School, and she was still teaching there when I was in college. We were living at 521 Southwest Sixtieth Court, in walking distance to a public elementary school named Fairlawn, a charming title that was contradicted by the grim day-to-day reality.

Still very plump, I became the object of severe teasing, which was made worse by the fact that I spoke with a decided Long Island accent. For the next few years, I tried my best to imitate the honeyed Southern twang of my Fairlawn classmates, but it was fairly hopeless. In sixth grade, I dreaded the gruesome practice called weigh-in day, when the children would be called forward by the school nurse, one by one, to step on the scale. As the nurse called out heartily, "Lorraine Viscardi: 100 pounds", the other children giggled, and hot blood flooded my cheeks in shame.

Years later, I would hear so many people complaining about the supposed cruelty of nuns in their childhood years. True, some sisters could be strict and, at times, grumpy, but I have to say that the only cruelty I recall came from physical education teachers, who did not wear habits or carry Rosary beads but instead wore chalk-white gym shorts and whistles dangling on lanyards around their necks. They failed to allow for physical differences among children and expected the fat kids to do everything the thin ones did. On days dedicated to that horrendous activity called "tumbling", I felt like a condemned prisoner facing the gallows. I can remember the sick feeling in my stomach as I stood in line, waiting my turn on the mat and praying that God would intervene to free me from having to do a forward roll. I did some of my most fervent praying then, as I beseeched God to drop a bomb on the playground or give me a heart attack, anything to spare me from the mat. Inevitably, my turn came and I failed miserably, while the class erupted in laughter.

I can't remember ever praying at home with my parents, except for the blessing that we said before meals. God and religion were topics that we just didn't talk about. In many ways, Catholicism to my parents was like water would be to fish. It was all around them, and they were completely immersed in it, especially in New York, where nearly everyone they knew was both Catholic and Italian. Why talk about being Italian when you are with Italians? And why talk about the water, unless someone takes it away from you?

Despite their reticence about religious discussions, my parents' actions revealed their deepest priorities. Saturday afternoon was reserved for confession, and we never missed Mass on Sunday, even when we had to rise very early because we had other events scheduled for the day. We didn't let a shred of meat touch our lips on Fridays, since that was the day that Jesus had died, and we made that sacrifice to show our love for him, just as we fasted during Lent.

It would be wrong, however, to conclude that our faith was simply a cluster of rules and regulations. Yes, the rules were important, because they had been handed down from generation to generation, and my parents respected tradition. But there was also awe and wonder in the Mass. We left the world behind when we entered the church, which was quiet, sweetly redolent of incense, and with tiny flames from votive candles piercing the darkness. At the moment of the Consecration, the bread and wine became the Body and Blood of Christ, which meant that we witnessed a miracle in every Mass. And since consecrated Hosts were always kept in the tabernacle, this meant that Christ was present there, and thus a Catholic church was truly God's house. In later years, when I ventured into Protestant churches, I was always dumbfounded by the lack of a tabernacle, because it seemed that the very heart of the church was missing.

If someone was very ill or if someone died, then the family went to church to say the Rosary. All of us were aware that we were not worshipping Mary, despite what critics might claim, but rather we were asking for her prayers. As for me, the relative for whom I most fervently prayed was Johnny Rosasco, my Aunt Rita's husband, who had died of a heart attack when their children were still babies. My favorite uncle, he had shown me how to use a spoon to pilfer juicy strawberries from a jar of jam, and I never forgot him.

When I heard about the poor souls in Purgatory who had no one to pray for them, I took it upon myself to say Rosaries on their behalf. And although no one said for sure whether or not animals were allowed into heaven, I couldn't imagine the place without them, so, just in case they also made a stopover in Purgatory, I prayed for my departed pet turtles, with a note scrawled on the back of a prayer card to remind me: "Pray for Flat-top and Wormy."

3

Impure Thoughts

In Miami, my father tried a series of different jobs and eventually settled on selling real estate, but our economic situation didn't seem to improve, since he was still struggling with his gambling problems. By the time I was ten, my relationship with him had become strained and painful. For some mysterious reason that still eludes me, I had developed an inner, negative voice that spat out sarcastic, bitter comments in my head, all directed at him.

True, my father gave his girls very little attention and wasn't the sole support of our family, failings that I surely had noticed, but the amount of resentment I harbored now seems out of proportion to his offenses. When he came home from work to announce that he had sold a piece of land, my sister and mother would join in the celebration, which usually included some impromptu dancing in the living room. My own memory, although foggy, has me standing on the sidelines, thinking sarcastic thoughts, and making some excuse so I wouldn't have to dance.

One day he didn't come home from work at the usual time, and my mother told us in tears that he'd had a heart attack and was in the hospital. I was stricken with a choking guilt, because I had a simplistic, cause-and-effect image of God and prayer and figured he was punishing me for my negativity. In bed at night, the bitter mental voice was silenced as tears ran in hot rivulets into my ears.

I blamed myself for my father's illness and began praying, hard, for his recovery. Fortunately, he did not die, but after he came home from the hospital, weak and thin, he began falling into frequent dark pits of depression. Before long, he was finding fault with Miami and longing for the familiarity of family and friends in New York.

The moving boxes showed up again, and during the summer following sixth grade, we boarded up the latest Miami house, packed our belongings, and headed to New York, where we lived in an apartment. That fall, I found myself back in Ascension Catholic School, with many of the same classmates I'd known in kindergarten and first grade. Just as we were settling back into life in New York and I was renewing my friendships, however, my parents decided they had made a mistake leaving Miami, and we returned. In the middle of the school year, I joined the other seventh graders at Saint Michael the Archangel Catholic School in Miami.

Some of the most dreaded words of my childhood were: "Class, today we have a new girl." The words, along with my weight, branded me as an outsider and a misfit, a category that haunted me for many years. By the time I began high school at Immaculata Academy, an all-girls Catholic school on Biscayne Bay, the family had moved to another house, but at least we stayed put long enough at 6090 Southwest Twelfth Street for me to graduate with my class.

Excited about starting high school, I recorded my goals in my diary, which I had named Tony, after my guardian angel: I wanted to someday get married, have loads of kids, and go to college, with the last one being the top priority.

There were many topics the diary didn't delve into, because of my fear that someone in the family would read it. There is no mention, for example, of the times when I seriously wondered if I had what the nuns called a "vocation to the religious life".

Was God calling me to become a nun? This was an extremely difficult question to answer, because I had certain qualities that might have suited me to convent life: my studiousness, my introversion, and my fierce shyness around boys. Other girls were showing interest in dating and begging their parents to go to dances, but not me. When I confessed this apparent failing to my mother, she assured me that I didn't have to be like the other girls because I was like her, and I would catch up with the other girls later, just as she had.

In my freshman year of high school, I began to stage a quiet rebellion by smoking cigarettes on the way to school, keeping this a secret from my parents. At those times, I was sure that God wasn't calling me to become a nun, because I simply couldn't imagine myself hunkering down and doing whatever a Mother Superior might say. Besides, if I became a nun, I would not be able to model my life after my mother's.

I was proud that my mother was a college graduate and a teacher, and I loved going to her classroom now and again, where I would clean the blackboards and fantasize about one day being a teacher too. Still, my feelings about my mother's job had a marked ambivalence, because I also longed for her to be a housewife. On days when she was not teaching, she always baked an apple pie, and the scent of cinnamon permeated the house like luscious incense. Even today, the taste of apple pie evokes my mother's yearning to stay home and my own sorrow that she couldn't get what she wanted.

❦

My best friend, Alice, and I managed to get into our share of trouble with the sisters at Immaculata Academy. We would puff away on our mentholated cigarettes in the girls' restroom, standing on the toilets so we could direct the smoke out the windows. The plan was simple: As soon as we detected a sister's presence, we would flush the cigarettes away and then exit the stalls innocently. But the principal, Sister Marie de Lourdes, was on to us. She waited patiently outside the stalls and then insisted on sniffing our breath for incriminating evidence.

Many Catholics of my generation have bitter memories of the sisters, because they were known to be strict, no-nonsense women. It is true that Sister Marie de Lourdes stalked the halls, looking for girls who committed misdemeanors, such as being absent from class without a pass or having smudges on their saddle oxfords. And it is also true that the nuns measured the length of our skirts to be sure we were achieving the required degree of modesty.

Although I was greatly annoyed at the time, in retrospect I believe they were trying to impress on us the existence of definite standards, which we had to live up to. I often rebelled against their rules and made fun of them behind their backs, but when I went to college and immediately landed in honors courses, I appreciated the depth of education that I had received under the sisters' watchful eyes.

They were very strict, but they were also quite human. One of the elderly nuns, Sister Saint John, one day announced to the class that she had a "true voice" and then, to demonstrate, launched into a wobbly, impromptu solo. Meanwhile, I sat at my desk, contemplating thoughts of death and disease to avoid bursting into raucous laughter. The younger nuns, Sister Mary Maurice and Sister Laurenza, were sweet and gentle-natured and often had a wry smile on their faces as they contemplated their teenage students.

With puberty in full swing, I became obsessed with avoiding what were called "impure thoughts", which I assumed never plagued the sisters, who seemed to be the very essence of purity. Of course, like the attempt to avoid thinking about an elephant, the more I tried to banish forbidden images, the more they reappeared. My impure thoughts centered on imagining passionate kisses that I might share with Elvis Presley, whom I planned to marry someday. Beyond that, I had a confused sense of what were called the "facts of life", since my mother was too embarrassed to discuss such things with her girls.

When I had turned thirteen, she had given me a pamphlet filled with colorful images of birds and butterflies, that tried to describe the process of reproduction. After reading it carefully, I knew the birds and butterflies were up to something, but I wasn't sure what. Of course, I was too shy to ask any questions, and my mother was loath to offer any explanations. For a long time, I was so baffled about sexuality that I thought babies emerged from women's belly buttons, since an aunt had mentioned once that they came out of an opening "down there". At some point, my classmates gleefully set me straight on the details about reproduction, and I found their descriptions shocking and implausible.

My sophomore-year diary describes a girl who liked to write poetry, swim, read, watch movies, cook, and go bowling. I wrote that I hated to do housework and sew and wanted to be a writer, a housewife, and, despite my apparent horror about the details of human sexuality, the mother of a dozen kids.

I was still somewhat chubby and fiercely embarrassed about my serious outbreaks of acne, but, with my mother's help,

I managed to land a date to the prom with Joe, her friend's son. A Catholic boy, he was tall and gangly and two years older than I, and he soon professed that he had fallen in love with me. Unfortunately, I didn't share his romantic feelings and was stunned when he sent me flowers and an accompanying note: "You'll get that dozen yet."

The thought of what I would have to do with this boy to get a dozen children utterly repelled me. However, we did engage in long, passionate kisses in his car. He tried his hardest to French kiss me, but I kept my teeth staunchly locked together. Back at home, I would anguish over whether or not we were committing mortal sins. He assured me that we were not, since all we ever did was kiss, but I was so scrupulous about everything and feared that my immortal soul might be in jeopardy. What if we had a car wreck after a session of necking and were killed? Were a few moments of pleasure worth an eternity of suffering?

Unfortunately, there was no one that I could turn to with this dilemma. The thought of discussing such topics with my parents—or the sisters—was beyond belief. I would be far too embarrassed, and they would not understand. The only way to remedy things, I was sure, was to amend my weekly list in the confessional to include: "I had impure thoughts one hundred times." Fortunately, the priests never bothered to interrogate me on this point, and I continued to hope that I would get to the confessional before dying in a car wreck and going to hell.

Years later, I discovered that mortal sins are actions that seriously injure our relationship with God. A mortal sin has to involve a very grave matter, such as murder or adultery, and must be committed with deliberate consent and with full knowledge of the wrongdoing. The sisters, bless their little wimples, hinted that kissing was a mortal sin, because they wanted to prevent the girls from doing things that might lead to something far more serious. But their tactics created an awful lot of guilty feelings in the most scrupulous girls and had no effect on the wilder ones.

Although times have changed greatly since then, in my senior year in high school, it seemed that all my friends were virgins. No one even talked about the loss of virginity, because we all assumed that was something that would happen on our wedding nights. The expressions we used in the innocent days prior to the sexual revolution revealed the general attitudes of society. "Getting in trouble" was something that every girl wanted to avoid, and the only way to do that was to remain a virgin. Having a child out of wedlock was considered a terrible disgrace, and no one wanted to be known as a "bad girl". All my friends had strict curfews, and many, like me, had fathers who waited at the door for them to return home.

There was a small group of girls in high school who were known to be "wild", which meant they wore too much makeup after school and hiked up the skirts of their uniforms to show their knees. When one girl from this crowd showed up in her senior year with a suspiciously large belly, rumors that she was pregnant began spreading throughout the school. But there was another story, which said that the poor girl was suffering from a tumor. I was innocent enough to believe the latter story, because I couldn't imagine that any girl would have sex before marriage. It would not be long, however, before my thoughts on this issue would definitely change.

4

Life in Sin City

The book shocked me right down to the carefully polished tips of my saddle oxfords. I was taking the bus home from high school when I stopped by a newsstand and saw *Why I Am Not a Christian* by Bertrand Russell. Had the title been *Why I Like to Kill People*, I would not have been more horrified. Little did I know that in a few short years, I would be reading Russell's diatribe and admiring it.

A little later, I told one of the sisters at Immaculata about my decision to attend the University of Florida in Gainesville. The poor woman's face turned as white as her wimple as she clutched the crucifix on her Rosary beads. Then, in no uncertain terms, she made her dire prediction: "If you go to a secular college, you will be in danger of losing your faith." I thought she was completely off the mark, but there would come a day when I would wonder if she possessed the power of prophecy.

In the summer of 1964, just a few months before departing for college, I met a man who seemed very much like the Prince Charming I had imagined for years. Richard was a blond, green-eyed Italian, the handsome brother of my friend Terri, and in his twenties. For the first time in my life, I felt a true physical longing for a man. To top it all off, this charming guy was Catholic, had a well-paying job, and seemed to think I was sweet and pretty.

When I went to college, we lost touch with each other, but over the years, I would look back and wonder: What if I had married him and stayed in Miami? What if I had lived a normal life, instead of the one that awaited me at the University of Florida? How many heartbreaks would I have avoided? How many children might I have had?

My sister decided to live an ordinary life. At eighteen, she married a boy named Richard H. Mende, who was in the military, and the twosome went to live in Turkey for two years. When we went to the airport to say good-bye to the newlyweds, I saw my father cry for the first time in my life. I was beginning to suspect that the man I regarded as distant and indifferent had a secret existence unknown to me.

My mom's big eyes shimmered with tears when she and my father deposited me in my room on the fourth floor of Broward Hall dormitory. She helped me unpack the color-coordinated outfits I had so carefully assembled: the pink and blue wraparound skirts, with matching blouses with Peter Pan collars. After so many years of wearing uniforms, the idea of donning "real" clothes was thrilling, and for the first year of college, I actually kept records of which outfits I wore on which days, so I would not wear the same thing too many times in a row.

My mother arranged the shoes carefully in the closet and plumped up the pillows on my bed, trying to forestall the inevitable, dreaded moment of our parting. My father waited outside, smoking a cigar and no doubt surveying the males on campus with suspicion. He had always grilled his daughters' prospective dates at the front door and had instituted early curfews. Now he surely must have felt uneasy as he realized that his younger daughter would be making her own dating decisions.

I was upset to see my parents get in the car and head down the highway home, but I was also quite anxious to start my new, adult life. Fortunately, my roommate, Trish, was a perfect match for me, because we shared the same wacky sense of humor. We were soon in fits of hysterics in the dining hall just a few hours after we'd met.

My freshman and sophomore years went by in a blur of parties, dates, drinking, exams, hangovers, term papers, and endless yearnings to find "Mr. Right". Many of the girls in Broward Hall rather quickly located the men of their dreams, while I was unwittingly perfecting the skill of going after "Mr. Wrong". It seemed I was constantly falling in love, getting my heart broken, recovering, and going on to the next man. I wanted to be like the other girls, but my old self-image as a misfit was haunting me. My friends jokingly referred to my dates as "Lorrie's weirdos", and they were often correct in their estimation.

Mark was one of the first boys I dated on campus. He was a wiry Jewish fellow with a quick, cynical sense of humor and a slightly mournful attitude toward life. He wined and dined me for a while, and just when I was beginning to suspect that he was "the one", he informed me that he could never take me home to meet his mother since I was not Jewish, and that was the end of that.

Before long, I was infatuated with Emilio, the darkly handsome Cuban-American graduate assistant in one of my English classes. His goal was to become a famous novelist, and after we had dated for a while, I secretly decided my goal was to become his wife. His one big fear was being drafted and sent to Vietnam, so he devised a clever, albeit bizarre, plan: He would eat himself into such a large clothing size that he would be unable to fit into a uniform. With this plan in mind, my beloved settled down each evening in Larry's Steak House on University Avenue, where he polished off three entrees and desserts, with me nearby, watching in amazement.

After a six-month whirlwind relationship, during which time we saw each other daily and I fell fiercely in love with him, Emilio informed me, out of the blue, that we were becoming "too serious". The news crushed me, especially because I was coming down with mononucleosis at the time and was quite ill. In any event, I never saw him again, and I don't know if he managed to evade the draft or not.

If Catholicism had been the water in which I had swum from my earliest years, Gainesville seemed like dry land. I had rarely encountered people who did not believe in God, and suddenly they were the stars of my college courses. As I delved into the writings of Marx, Nietzsche, Camus, and Freud, I started seriously to doubt, and then I finally abandoned my childhood faith. Obviously, there were many Catholic students who encountered the same classroom teachings that I did, and remained faithful to their religion, but I equated becoming an adult with turning my back on God.

One of my first honors English courses was called "The Loss of Innocence", an ironically apt title, given the experiences that lay in store for me in Gainesville. I remember how angry my father was when he discovered the course title and how I assured him that there were many kinds of innocence besides the one he no doubt was thinking of—which, by the way, we never mentioned, since we never used the word "sex" in our home.

In truth, though, my father was correct, because the course did include novels featuring sexual experimentation, with the unquestioned assumption being that such behavior was an acceptable part of growing up. The protagonists of the novels I was reading lost their innocence, along with their faith, and my professors expressed no surprise or regret over either occurrence.

In 1962, a Catholic writer named Flannery O'Connor had written a letter to a freshman in college who feared that he was losing his faith. Her advice would have helped me tremendously, had I only known about it: "If you want your faith, you have to work for it", she wrote. "For every book you read that is anti-Christian, make it your business to read one that presents the other side of the picture." [1]

She also went on to say something that would have surely shocked many of my professors, who put religious faith in the same category as superstition: "Don't think you have to abandon reason to be a Christian." [2] She emphasized that faith was more valuable and mysterious and immense than anything that this young man would learn in college, and she advised him to cultivate what she called Christian skepticism: "It will keep you free ... to be formed by something larger than your own intellect or the intellects of those around you." [3]

One thing was for certain. At the University of Florida in the sixties, many professors and students believed there could be nothing larger than their own intellects. Ironically, many of the authors I was studying in my English classes were either Catholics or heavily influenced by Catholicism, but most professors skirted these facts. If they did happen to note an author's belief in God, it was nearly always handled with a smirk, as if theism were some quaint habit that sophisticated adults would do well to break.

The hippie generation was being born, and I was eager to join the throng of rebels. In short order, my Rosary beads gave way to love beads, and my crucifix was replaced by a peace symbol. In high school, the sisters had drummed the ideal of modesty into the girls and insisted that their skirts should hang a certain number of inches below their knees. Now I was going braless and wearing dresses that resembled long blouses. Virginity had been highly prized in high school, but with the sexual revolution in full swing, it became an embarrassment.

I became the poster child for the "tune in, turn on, drop out" generation, although I never gave any serious thought to really dropping out of college. Somehow, despite my wild social life, which included drinking binges and puffing on pungent, hand-rolled, and quite illegal cigarettes, I eventually managed to graduate with honors and was even elected to Phi Beta Kappa.

Moving to an apartment complex known as "Sin City", which I did in my junior year, was probably not the smartest move. Fortunately, my parents thought the place was called by its ordinary name, University Gardens, and figured I'd be safe with my three female roommates. What my parents didn't know was that my French professor also lived in Sin City and was the latest in a long line of "Lorrie's weirdos". I was nineteen, and he was twenty-six and a heavy drinker, but that only made him more worldly and intriguing to me.

He was the first man with whom I had a sexual relationship, and although at first he resisted the advances of his much-younger student, I think he eventually concluded that he might as well enjoy the fling. As for me, I was starry-eyed and once again in love, and I figured that we would one day marry. It was a classic case of mixed signals. I was bewitched by hippie propaganda, which urged young people to liberate themselves from the restrictions of the past. Free-roaming sex was seen as one obvious ticket to liberation, since our parents' generation had preached commitment and marriage. Feminist propaganda also urged women to make the first move instead of waiting for men to call them. It was a very confusing time for both genders, and I am sure that many men didn't know what to make of supposedly "liberated" women, who were quite different from the girls of their high school days. It would take me quite a few years to realize that the notion of "free love" was a huge lie.

Not surprisingly, guys seemed to be the ones reaping the main benefits of bed hopping. Many "hip" women were trying their best to imitate male behavior, because the women's liberation movement, also under way, assured them there were no innate differences between the sexes. The solution seemed simple enough: Women had to change their behavior to free themselves from the past. Invariably, though, when my girlfriends and I became emotionally attached to the men we were dating, they accused us of being "old-fashioned" because we were yearning for something more than a physical relationship.

I eventually became thoroughly disenchanted with the French professor's excessive drinking and stopped seeing him. Over the next few years, I repeated the same sad pattern time and time again. I would fall for a handsome, bright man and expect the relationship to develop into something serious. Many men were not seeking long-term relationships at all, however, and were merely enjoying spontaneous flings. I wanted to find a man to love and cherish me and to marry me, but I couldn't seem to realize that sex wouldn't get me there.

When I went home for college breaks, I attended Mass with my parents and acted like a dutiful daughter. To me, God, religion, and prayer were looking increasingly outdated, like my stuffed animals and tea sets, but I hid my new, "liberated" self from my parents. It wasn't that I was ashamed, I assured myself; it was just that they would never understand.

It would be unfair to claim that all my professors were atheists and agnostics, but a fairly large number of nonbelievers did seem to be teaching liberal arts courses. As I encountered professors who were either openly hostile to religion or completely indifferent to it, I became convinced that my Catholic faith was a ridiculous relic of my childhood.

Still, I must add a disclaimer: The professors certainly were not to blame for my loss of faith, since many students entered the classrooms of agnostics and atheists and came out with their beliefs intact. No one forced his beliefs upon me. My reasoning was childish, perhaps, but understandable: I was extremely impressed by my professors, who had doctorates in literature, psychology, science, and history, and figured that they must know something about faith that I did not.

More to the point, though, if there were no God, then was I not more free to pursue my wild lifestyle in Sin City? If God did not actually exist, I would no longer have to worry about committing mortal sins and going to hell. In a very odd turnaround, the girl who had once been so scrupulous about the smallest faults now was doing things that her former self would not have been permitted even to think about.

Did I ever feel guilty for turning my back on God? Did I ever wonder if I was making a huge mistake with enormous consequences? Unfortunately, my memory draws a blank with these questions. All I knew was that I had finally grown up, and even if I was often miserable because of the way men were treating me, I figured that my agonizing over their behavior was just part of adulthood.

At the time I thought of myself as a nonconformist, with my tie-dyed dresses and my eagerness to dabble in drugs and participate in antiwar demonstrations. Looking back, though, I have to wonder if perhaps the real nonconformists were the kids that the hippies jokingly called the "straights". These students continued going to church, avoided drugs, dated one person, and eventually got married. The hippies sneered at such conventional approaches to life, but when I calculate the terrible cost of our adventures, it seems that the "straights" had found the better path.

One friend, Toby, never got a chance to get older and reflect on his weird years in Gainesville. He was a very sensitive and intense guy who unfortunately had ingested too many hits of LSD and always seemed a little confused. One day he came to my apartment and asked me to shave all the hair off his head. To this day, I can still remember how he shivered as I spread the shaving cream and how surprised I was by the little bumps on his scalp. A few months later, he killed himself by jumping off a bridge in Jacksonville.

Today I hope I would notice the signs of a friend's increasing descent into mental illness, but given all the eccentric people in Gainesville back then, this gentle, but tortured, fellow seemed like one of the crowd. I have never forgotten him, and I still pray for the repose of that young soul.

5

Vendetta against God

My parents expected me to return home after I graduated from college with my degree in English, but I was loath to live under their keen eyes and curfews once again. After all, I had drunk deeply from the well of liberation, and I wanted to continue sampling the free-wheeling lifestyle that Gainesville offered.

I also was hungry to collect more degrees and somewhat reluctant to look for a job in the "real" world. When I told my parents that I wanted to enroll in a master's degree program in English, they were delighted. Getting a master's degree had been one of my mother's unfulfilled dreams, and she wanted that for me. By 1972, I had landed that degree and was still longing for something more. The idea of being a college professor intrigued me, so I decided to embark on a doctoral program in philosophy.

In so many ways, the philosophy department seemed like the perfect place for me to settle. It offered an array of brilliant professors and quirky students, most of them male and many of them single, along with enticing subject matter. There were also incredible parties, where students and faculty drank themselves into oblivion while debating the finer points of Kant's *Critique of Pure Reason* and Husserl's theory of phenomenology. At one especially memorable party, graduate students and faculty members frolicked under the live oak trees and sipped glasses of wine, without a stitch of clothing on. When I look back at those days, I am utterly astonished that I failed to notice that what we were doing was bizarre. In all fairness, there was a handful of graduate students and faculty who walked the straight-and-narrow path, but, for the vast majority, old-fashioned notions of right and wrong had simply flown out the window with the hippie movement.

Although I'd given up on religion, I was fascinated with philosophy, since one of my big interests was figuring out the meaning of life. I knew that philosophy came from the Greek words *philo* and *sophia*, meaning love of wisdom, but I never considered the fact that the religion I had rejected presented quite a wise and loving picture of ultimate reality.

As a child, I'd been taught to find life's meaning in knowing, loving, and serving God, but now I believed that the world had come into existence by pure accident and there was no higher being to love and serve. In 1955, Flannery O'Connor had aptly described the world as a place where "you breathe in nihilism." She had gone on to say that, without the Church to fight it, she would have been "the stinkingest logical positivist you ever saw".[1]

As for logical positivists, they were rampant in the philosophy department. These were the folks who staunchly maintained that statements were meaningless unless they could be verified by sensory experience. Obviously, this was a clever, albeit severely flawed, way to eliminate claims about God, not to mention abstract terms like truth, beauty, and goodness.

The nihilists claimed everything happened by chance and people were simply stumbling along in a godless universe, trying to create their own meaning out of chaos. Such was the belief of atheistic existentialists like Jean-Paul Sartre, who became my new guru. In many ways, the whole hippie movement was based on nihilism, because it was generally accepted that people had to find their own way, since there was no God to give the universe a higher meaning. In the absence of God, there were no absolute values; one could just as well cherish beauty as ugliness, which might explain some of the art of the day. Oddly enough, though, even atheists must have faith in something, as Tolstoy pointed out: "Without believing that life is worth living, we would not live."[2] Unfortunately, I wasn't aware of this point in the heyday of my own spiritual rebellion.

ॐ

Shortly after I enrolled in the graduate program in philosophy, I began living with David, a graduate student who drove a beat-up Volkswagen Beetle and had, like me, thoroughly rejected his Catholic roots. We lived in a run-down cabin on a lake a few miles from town, with my gray-and-white tomcat, Funky, and the occasional possum family that wandered into the kitchen at night to pilfer cat food.

One night, we decided to experiment with LSD. I was extremely nervous about the idea, given what I had heard about people who experienced "bad trips" and never returned to reality. But friends who were seasoned users promised huge personal insights and revelations, so I caved in. Fortunately, we took our "trip" in a safe place, among people whom we trusted. Still, as the framed portraits on the walls came to life and started talking to me, I began hoping for the journey to end. Once the experience was over, we all declared it very important and meaningful, but I was smart enough to realize how easily it could have turned into a grim nightmare, and I never again ventured into the world of hallucinogens.

David was a studious and affectionate man, and after we had lived together awhile, he declared that he wanted to marry me. He seemed truly to cherish me, despite all my flaws and my considerably checkered past. I was still searching for my storybook version of Prince Charming, however, and I was afraid to marry this guy because he struggled with some dark emotional demons.

He was the one who answered the phone call from my sister and later tenderly broke the news to me that shattered my complacent world of philosophical debates and wild parties. My mother had been diagnosed with breast cancer and was facing a mastectomy. I will never forget the way I cried in my lover's arms that afternoon. It was at that moment that life came crashing down on me and I knew that I would never be the same.

My mother had retired from teaching when she'd turned sixty, and she'd been diagnosed with cancer shortly after that. Instead of the glorious retirement years she'd dreamed of, she went on to endure long, painful bouts of surgery, chemotherapy, and radiation. As for me, I fell into denial about the seriousness of her illness and kept expecting the treatments to take care of the problem.

Her doctors offered some hope at first, and when the situation worsened, my parents were careful to filter the information, so they would not upset their daughters. Still, I am appalled at my apparent blindness. Even when my father told me, in December 1975, that my mother needed an oxygen tank in the bedroom to help her breathe, I still believed she would get better.

If I could step into a time machine, I would switch the dial to 1972 and drop out of graduate school. I would head to Fort Lauderdale, where my parents had moved, and spend my mother's final days with her, going to the beach and shopping, two of her favorite activities. It is still heartbreaking to me that she kept a room in their condo ready for the day when I would move back, but I was too wrapped up in my own world to realize that the room would not be there forever.

I was continuing my frenzied search for Prince Charming, the man who would tie up all the raggedy ends of my life. When I fell in love with Ted, a philosophy professor, David and I suffered a rather ugly breakup, and I took Funky to establish residence in an apartment at 620 Northeast Boulevard, near the Gainesville duck pond. To this day, I regret the selfish and cruel way that I treated that kind and considerate man.

I was growing disenchanted with philosophy but continued moving toward my goal of getting a doctorate. If the truth be told, many passages in Hegel, Kant, and Heidegger at times seemed like total nonsense. Still, I dutifully plowed through the readings and even churned out a paper on Husserl that was published in a journal, despite my growing suspicion that the stuff I was writing would appear as gibberish to any ordinary person.

If the philosophy students or professors believed in God, they kept this fact to themselves. Trying to defend the existence of God, say, at a party, would instigate a convoluted debate with an analytical philosopher, who would demand to know just what you meant by the words "existence" and "God". The Marxists would chime in that mankind had invented God, and the feminists would insist that God was part of a masculine plot designed to keep women in their place. Little wonder that no one wanted to defend theism. To do so risked being subject to serious scrutiny and mockery, because nearly everyone agreed that God was an antiquated construct. My friends and I considered ourselves much too worldly and rational for churchgoing and prayer. Religion, we believed in our arrogant way, was something for the less sophisticated and less rational people of the world.

My attitude toward prayer changed, however, when I finally realized the gravity of my mother's condition. At some point toward the end of her life, I started an odd bargaining with the God in whom I no longer believed. I figured there was just the slimmest chance that he did exist, and, if so, he might grant my request. Besides, I would have done anything to save my mother, and that included acting in contradiction to my professed atheism. And so, in an odd jumble of emotions, I prayed for her miraculous recovery and promised God that if he would cure her, I would come back to him. In retrospect, it seems clear that some vestiges of my belief in God were lurking in my heart. I turned to prayer in my hour of need, not to other things that I had branded irrational, such as superstitions or good-luck charms. Prayer was the one thing that I felt might help my mother.

I flew down to Fort Lauderdale on January 6, 1976, after a phone call from my father that left little doubt about the seriousness of my mother's condition. Looking drawn and worried, he met me at the airport and drove me immediately to the hospital, where she was lying in bed, breathing with great difficulty.

I was coming down with a cold that was turning into bronchitis. As always, my mother expressed joy in seeing me, but she became concerned when she noticed that I was coughing. She asked me to bend down and then kissed my forehead, the same way she had when I was little, to see if I had a temperature. Then she instructed my father to take me back to their condo so I could get some rest. I was struck at that time with how compassionate and selfless she was, even though she was clearly suffering.

The next morning, while it was still dark, I heard the door of the condo opening and my father returning from the hospital. He awakened me in tears to tell me that my mother had died during the night. Her roommate at the hospital told him she had seen very bright lights during the night, and she was certain that they were not the overhead lights. "The angels came to take your mother home", said my father.

The tears that were unleashed, the sorrow that flooded out of me, the anguish that shredded my soul were indescribable. I cried until I had no tears left, and my eyes swelled to three times their size. The fact that she was gone—the little dark-eyed woman who called me "Lorrainee" and signed her notes with hearts, the woman whom I had worshipped since childhood—was impossible to believe. I opened her closet and hugged her dresses, hungry for her scent. I knew my life would never be the same without her.

As for God, I swore that I would never, ever have anything to do with him. He could have performed a miracle but had failed to do so. Just as my father had not provided for the family when I was a child and had not helped make my mother's dream of staying home come true, God the Father had betrayed me in my hour of need.

As I mentioned earlier, my grandfather Antonio Bibbo had bitterly turned his back on Catholicism after seeing the village priest frolicking with a woman. Unconsciously following in his footsteps, I took my mother's death as sufficient reason to return, with great fervor, to atheism. More than that, I decided to launch an actual vendetta against God. I was so embittered that, when I began teaching philosophy to college students as naïve as I once had been, I did my best to convince them that God did not exist.

❦

My sister was still a faithful Catholic, and at the time of our mother's death, she and her husband, Dick, had two children: Ricky, seven, and Jennifer Grace, barely two. These little ones had been the true lights in my mother's dark journey with cancer. There was nothing that pleased my mother so much as a visit from Jennifer and Ricky, who showed up in the condo with coloring books and crayons and spent the afternoon with her. Toward the end of her life, my mother's letters were peppered liberally with detailed descriptions of what her beloved grandchildren were doing.

Rosemary told me, in whispered tones, that her house had filled with the scent of roses on the day of our mother's death. She also hinted, as I choked back bitter retorts, that death was not the final word in a Christian's journey and that our mother was in a better place. I was well aware that mysterious reports about roses were linked to miraculous appearances of the Virgin Mary, but I refused to give any credence to my sister's experience.

Silently, I chalked up her words to her emotional distress, and later, when I was teaching philosophy, I used her experience as part of my vendetta against God. In exploring reports of mystical events, including visual, auditory, and olfactory phenomena, I explained to my students that such claims were simply manifestations of mental disturbances. Nothing could be interpreted in a transcendent way, I emphasized, since nothing beyond the material world existed.

6

The Feminist Creed

I gritted my teeth during the sermon at my mother's funeral Mass at Blessed Sacrament Church in Fort Lauderdale, especially when Father Jerome Martin mentioned that she was in a place where she was no longer suffering. I also ignored comments from well-meaning relatives about "the will of God". Since I did not believe in an afterlife, I stood by her graveside at the Queen of Heaven cemetery and bid her a tearful goodbye. I was sure that my mother no longer existed and that I would never see her again under any circumstances.

After the funeral, I returned to Gainesville and tried to stir up interest in my studies, but I was severely depressed. As the days passed, I kept waiting for the phone to ring and to hear my mother assuring me that it had all been a mistake, or some horrible joke, and she was still alive. I longed to hear her chirping, "Hi, Honey!" on the line. It was simply impossible to think that I would never hear that voice again.

Her death shifted the dynamics in our family. She had been the communicator, who wrote long, detailed letters and chatted with me at length on the phone. Usually, if I called home and my father answered, we would discuss the weather for a while, and then he would ask: "Do you want to talk with your mother?"

Although my relationship with my father was strained, it seemed that he had been making great headway with befriending my sister's children even before my mother died. The photos show him carrying Ricky at the beach and playfully sharing his Panama hat with him. On the night Jennifer was born, my father rushed to the hospital at 3 A.M. to see her. Later, when she was eleven months old, my mother had written, "Jennifer not only dances but claps her hands while Daddy sings the *tarantella!*"

Now my father started taking up the letter-writing slack, and for the first time in my life, I began to feel close to him. He wrote me weekly, each letter penned heavily in dark ink on sheets from a yellow legal pad and often accompanied by a check, with the joking admonition to avoid spending the money all in one place. In one letter, he cautioned me to be more careful with my curling iron, as I had reported to him that I had accidentally burned Funky's tail. In another, after I sent him a stack of photos, he commented that the old cat was quite photogenic.

When I visited my father in Fort Lauderdale, I would bake chocolate chip cookies and biscotti and store them in the freezer for him. Many of his letters mention the "delicious munchies" and how grateful he was for them. In his letters he took joy in telling me the news about the grandchildren: Jennifer had lost a brand-new shoe and apparently enjoyed playing in the toilet bowl. Ricky made his First Holy Communion. "I gave him a cross and chain to wear around his neck. He was very happy to have it."

I don't remember my father ever telling me I was pretty when I was growing up, but now he wrote that he really liked my new hairdo, adding, "You are a pretty girl, whether your hair is long or short. Don't forget it."

At the end of each letter, my normally reticent father jotted down a long string of Xs and Os to represent kisses and hugs. One letter had thirty-four of these by his signature, revealing that perhaps he was more affectionate than I had imagined. "Take care of yourself", he wrote, and signed the letter, "My loving affection to you."

On the first Palm Sunday after my mother's death, my father visited the cemetery and left palms on her grave. In his letter, he reminded me that our family had always exchanged palms, and he enclosed one for me. "I miss her so much", he wrote, underlining each word. "It seems each day that passes makes it more difficult to accept the fact that she is no longer here."

My father loved traveling, and he and my mother had taken a trip to Europe before her illness made her housebound. Two months after her death, my father invited me to go on a four-day cruise to the Bahamas with him. We sailed on a huge Italian ship on March 15, 1976, and I was stunned by the sumptuous meals and elegant surroundings. Still, everywhere we went, I had this nagging sensation that something was wrong and someone was missing. One night, I found my poor dad, sitting alone on a deck chair and weeping into his big handkerchief. He and my mother had always been the proverbial two peas in a pod, and now, he confessed, he missed her terribly.

A few months later, he wrote me about his plans to take another cruise on a boat named *Italia*, which would go to Puerto Rico, Saint Thomas, Martinique, Venezuela, Aruba, and Colombia. He would depart from Port Everglades on July 6, 1976, and return on July 17. He was planning to buy new clothes for the trip, he wrote, and promised to send cards from each port he visited. And, of course, he would call me as soon as he returned.

On July 6, the phone rang, and it was my sister. Evidently, my father had suffered a heart attack in the condo and died, with his bags neatly packed for the cruise. Although it seemed impossible, I was now departing for Fort Lauderdale to attend the second funeral in six months. I mourned the premature closing of this chapter in my life, the one in which my father and I were finally developing a real relationship.

My emotions were oddly jumbled at his funeral. I went from an absolute certainty that there could not possibly be a God, given the suffering in the world, especially my own, to the suspicion that perhaps God did exist but was intent on punishing me for all the bad things I'd done. In either case, my heart was completely hardened against religion, and I bit my tongue when one aunt tried to make sense of this latest tragedy in our lives by saying, "Gracie called him home."

My father was buried in the new suit he had purchased for the cruise and went to rest in the Queen of Heaven cemetery, next to my mother's grave. After the funeral, there was another big shock in store for my sister and me. As we were cleaning out our father's car, we found a crumpled, black-and-white photo in the glove compartment. It showed him as a young man with a little blond girl perched affectionately on his lap. We knew that she was not any of our cousins, so we asked his sister if she could identify the child. "Oh, didn't you know?" Aunt Mary replied, and then dropped the bombshell: "That's his first daughter. Your father was married before he met your mother."

Now my spool of childhood memories started crazily to unwind. If there had been a secret daughter, what other hidden facts might exist that my sister and I would never know about? And why had our parents concealed the truth from us for so long? Of course, I realized that divorce, especially among Catholics, had been a terrible disgrace in my parents' day, but I fretted for a long time about my parents hiding the identity of my father's first child. Although I felt betrayed and terribly confused by this discovery, I eventually realized that I had no grounds to complain about deception. After all, my parents had been unaware that their quiet, honors-student daughter had been harboring a secret identity for years.

They hadn't known that during the Vietnam War protests, I had been among the crowd of rowdy students being chased down University Avenue by the National Guard. They hadn't known that I agreed with Karl Marx's claim that religion was the opiate of the people, or that I had turned my back on all the Catholic training they had instilled in me. And they certainly hadn't known about my long string of romances.

I had assured myself that I had good reasons to deceive my parents: I didn't want to hurt them with the truth, and I also feared their disapproval. After a while, I realized that my rationalizations were probably similar to their reasons for concealing the divorce and the first daughter's identity from Rosemary and me.

❦

When I returned to Gainesville after my father's funeral, I was weary and exhausted and longing to see Ted, whom I had been dating for three years. Little did I know that a snake was about to lunge.

As we began eating dinner in a candle-lit gourmet restaurant, Ted casually mentioned that he had engaged in a one-night stand while I was attending my father's funeral. I think he expected me to laugh this off as no big deal, but instead, my heart turned to ice in my chest, and I stormed out of the restaurant, with the meal untouched. Even when he apologized profusely and proposed marriage to me a few months later, my feelings remained frozen.

I'm sure I was an enigma to the men I was dating. I paid serious lip service to the dogmas of freethinking feminism and tried to give the impression of being a "liberated" woman. In truth, though, I had plenty of old-fashioned expectations when it came to romance, and I demanded fidelity from my boyfriends.

Reflecting on my life in Gainesville and all the broken relationships, I have to wonder: Was I looking for a man to replace God in my life? I wanted someone to save me from myself, to love me unconditionally, to cherish me, and to be faithful to me forever. I couldn't figure out what I was doing wrong. Many traditional-minded women in college had found husbands, but the freethinkers like me, who had gleefully abandoned the old rules and expectations, kept falling on their faces.

The birth control pill, which made its debut during my college years, seemed like the perfect solution for people who wanted sex without responsibility. The problem was that no one seemed to have factored in the emotional fall-out of sex without commitment. I saw evidence, time and again, in myself and other women, of the fact that men and women were hard-wired very differently when it came to sex and love. Generally, it seemed that many men were able to enjoy the free-wheeling, free-love lifestyle, while most women continued to yearn for commitment in their relationships. The pill might lessen the chances of pregnancy, but it could not change the emotional expectations in a woman's heart when she becomes intimate with a man. Still, at the time, feminists hailed the pill as a marvelous innovation that would change the world. Now sex could be even more spontaneous, since a woman on the pill could jump eagerly into bed with a man she had just met, without the unnecessary encumbrance of contraceptive devices. The pill changed a woman's cycle and had numerous unpleasant and unhealthy side effects, such as headaches, nausea, depression, and even (if you read the fine print on the package insert) the potential for blood clots and cancer. But women in their twenties tend to think they will live forever, and just as I told myself I would stop smoking "someday", I promised myself that the pill was just a temporary measure.

As I started to consider a research topic for my dissertation, I was strongly drawn to the feminist writings of Simone de Beauvoir, a disciple of Sartre. She preached liberation, self-definition, and women's need to escape from the societal shackles that tied them to the past. She thought of children as burdens and suggested that full-time motherhood was an inherently inferior pursuit, while having a job was a necessary prerequisite for a fulfilling life. Sex without commitment was part of the package of liberation.

Despite my own personal experiences to the contrary, I was intrigued by the feminist belief that the emotional and psychological differences between women and men were strictly the result of conditioning and thus could be changed. According to atheists like de Beauvoir, there could be no deeply rooted, God-given differences in masculine and feminine natures. After all, how could such differences exist when there was no God?

Even as I began research for my dissertation on de Beauvoir, I continued unconsciously to break nearly every feminist rule in my expectations about relationships. I wanted a long-term, committed relationship that would lead to marriage. I wanted a man to take care of me. Even if I seemed the feminist par excellence, with my advanced degrees, my own apartment, and my stacks of women's liberation tomes, in my heart I was still that girl in high school who was searching for Prince Charming.

I did not see it then, but de Beauvoir's claims about the prerequisites for women's happiness ran completely counter to my own mother's experiences. After all, my mother had enjoyed many privileges that de Beauvoir and other feminists promised would make women happy and fulfilled, such as a college education and a job, but she had lamented missing the chance to do the one thing that feminists insisted was unfulfilling: staying home and raising her children and being an ordinary, unassuming homemaker.

7

The Mist of Tears

A few months after my parents' deaths, I found myself in a relationship with another Mr. Wrong. He was attractive and witty but thoroughly self-centered, and I was reading his signals all wrong. I was yearning, more than ever, for the security of marriage, while he was simply enjoying a fling. One night at my apartment, we were drinking excessive amounts of Amaretto and getting thoroughly drunk when he casually mentioned another woman whom he was seeing. Flying into a rage, I screamed at him to leave my apartment, which he quickly did. I then grabbed a nearby bottle of Valium and emptied the contents into my mouth.

Fortunately, a dear friend who lived downstairs heard me weeping and drove me to the hospital. The nurse who took care of me that night assured me that no man was ever worth suicide and also mentioned that God had given me a second chance. I didn't want to disagree with someone so kind and attentive, but I felt that the credit went fully to the friend who had rescued me.

I was extremely drunk when I took those pills, so afterward I assured myself that I had not seriously wanted to end my life but instead had been furious with myself for getting dragged down by another empty relationship. I wasn't ready to draw a more obvious conclusion: The suicide attempt was based on something much deeper, namely, my belief that life with a capital *L* had no inherent meaning. In this framework, the meaning of my own life was something that I had to create, moment by moment, day by day, and the values I chose were purely arbitrary. Sadly, for a person who rejects a belief in God, there can be no deep-seated justification for saying that suicide is a bad thing, because with this mind-set, human actions are just random choices. One can kill oneself or not, and since all values are relative, the truly honest atheist would have to admit: "Well, they are both choices." I had been raised, of course, to believe that suicide was a terrible act of despair and that no situation could warrant it, but in giving up on God, I had also rejected the commandment that prohibited killing.

I was exhausted for a few days after the attempt, and experienced an unusual sense of peace as I was recovering. Friends brought me cookies and flowers and sat by my bedside, just spending time with me. I no longer cared about term papers or reports or deadlines, because these all seemed so trivial compared with what had almost happened to me. I didn't realize it, of course, but in truth I put a high value on living and was extremely relieved that I was still alive. I felt very grateful for a second chance, but I did not thank God but rather the friend who had taken me to the hospital.

All the rage and grief seemed to have vanished from my heart, and I felt hopeful about the future. Looking back, I believe my feelings of contentment and peacefulness were signals from God, who was trying to get my attention, although I had grown quite practiced in ignoring him. Sometimes I think about Francis Thompson's poem "The Hound of Heaven" when I recall my years in Gainesville:

I fled Him, down the nights and down the days;
I fled Him down the arches of the years;
I fled Him down the labyrinthine ways
Of my own mind; and in the mist of tears
I hid from Him. . . .[1]

The Hound was pursuing me, and wooing me, and nipping gently at my heels, but I had blinders on and refused to turn around and take a look. Even though I had been brought to the precipice and rescued, I never uttered a single prayer of gratitude to the One from whom I was hiding. I wonder if the nurse in that hospital prayed for me, because she surely recognized a soul lost "in the mist of tears" when she saw one.

Not too surprisingly, once I was fully recovered emotionally from the trauma of the suicide attempt, I fell in love again. This time, I came close to marrying Prince Charming and actually riding off into the sunset with him. Daniel was a philosophy graduate student, a tall, husky man with jet-black hair and eyes, a mellow Southern accent, and a wry sense of humor. He had also been raised Catholic, although his years studying philosophy had taken the edge off his faith.

We were both wounded. I was still grieving for my parents, and his brother had just died. Wrapped in this man's protective arms, I felt that I had finally met the one who would complete me on a deep, mystical level. What joy it was when this soul mate bought me an engagement ring. What ecstasy when we wove a tapestry of dreams about our future together. And what sorrow when, a few months later, I discovered the secret he had been concealing: My lover already had a sweetheart back home. Without much discussion, I showed up at Daniel's apartment one morning and handed him back the ring. The breakup was especially painful because he had been a friend as well as a lover, and I missed him on both accounts. Before long, though, I was on to a new adventure: I spotted an ad in a New Age journal for a Tibetan Buddhist retreat center in Wingdale, New York. The center was called "Maitri", which meant loving kindness, and the prospect of encountering such a treasure was very tempting to me.

On a whim, I made arrangements to go on a short retreat. Over the years, I had dabbled a bit in Eastern thought and had tried, without much success, to practice various forms of meditation. At this point in my life, it is little wonder that I had a special attraction to the first noble truth of Buddhism: "Life is suffering."

At the retreat center, novices and experienced Buddhists alike arose early and headed over to what was called the "shrine room", which was nestled in the woods in a lovely oasis of silence. There we sat cross-legged for hours, watching the inevitable procession of thoughts across our mental screens. The goal was to tag these unruly stampedes as "thinking" and turn one's attention back to breathing. With sufficient dedication and practice, one supposedly would learn to detach oneself from one's thoughts and memories, and eventually reach a stage where suffering would cease.

As for me, I enjoyed the Buddhists' wonderful vegetarian cooking and the delightful conversations with my fellow seekers, but it was agonizing to sit with my painful parade of memories, and there were times when I wanted to run screaming from the room. After meditation, there were long chanted prayers to various deities, the ringing of bells, and other rituals, but I could not find even a moment's release from my suffering. I was in far too much mental anguish over my latest broken relationship and my parents' deaths to benefit much from time spent in silence. In my journal, I wrote, "I feel like a tour guide who has hauled a pack of tourists over the same terrain too many times—in this case my own threadbare mental scenery."

The Buddhists were strict vegetarians and did not believe in killing anything, a principle that I found enticing at first. After a few days, however, the fly population was building up in the dining room to a degree that I found distressing. One evening, after the Buddhists had gone to bed, I enlisted the help of another fellow retreatant, and together we decimated the fly population. The next morning at breakfast, the sound of buzzing was distinctly absent, and if the Buddhists noticed, they were too kind to say a word.

When I returned to Gainesville, I felt that my life was at the proverbial crossroads. My interest in philosophy was definitely waning, and I was yearning to get on with what I thought of as life in the "real world". For me, that meant a husband, a home, and a job. I began dating Chris, a pleasant local fellow who was upbeat and congenial and who was intrigued by dating a graduate student. We had many differences, especially his lack of a bachelor's degree and his fascination with blues singers, but I was lonely, and I was twenty-nine, the age my mother had been when she married. And so, when he proposed, I said yes.

We were married by a justice of the peace in an outdoor setting, and then, on a whim, we moved to Albuquerque, where we took up residence with Funky in an old pink trailer on Blake Road. I had become so disenchanted with philosophy that I couldn't bear the thought of actually writing a dissertation, so I dropped out of the program.

In Albuquerque, I quickly found a job as a legal assistant, but my new husband had a tough time keeping a job, and before long, we began squabbling over money. In the midst of agonizing over the latest apparent mistake in my romantic life, I received a phone call from my brother-in-law, Dick, who jubilantly announced the birth of his third child, Christina Michelle. It was a reminder that my sister, who had dated exactly two men in her life and married one of them, was living a happy life that still seemed to evade me.

Desert life wasn't for us, so before long Chris and I moved to Smyrna, right outside Atlanta, and there we rented a basement apartment. We had hoped his job prospects would improve, but the situation only worsened, and as our sparring over money and other matters intensified, I fell into a serious depression. I hated to admit it, but this marriage had been a terrible mistake. Despite Chris' protests and promises that things would improve, I packed up my belongings and moved out. We divorced a few months later.

I began teaching English and philosophy on a part-time basis at Georgia Tech, and Funky and I settled into an apartment located in an old house at 546 Ridgecrest Road in Atlanta. The landlord and his wife, Mr. and Mrs. Spruill, lived downstairs with a dog named Happy, which I took to be a good sign.

❧

The first day at Georgia Tech, I was having trouble finding the classroom and spotted a likely room filled with students, mostly male, so I peered inside and inquired, "Is this Philosophy 101?" Years later, I discovered that one of the students, Jeffrey Patrick Murray, had turned to another and jokingly said, "I'll bet that was the teacher."

The students evidently expected a dour, bearded man with a pipe to show up as their philosophy instructor, so they were probably surprised when a curly-haired Italian-looking lady, wearing a brown suede outfit with matching cowboy boots, walked into the room and introduced herself as Lorraine Viscardi, their new teacher. My eyes swept over the room and lit upon a particularly handsome guy with green eyes, dark brown hair, and a well-trimmed beard. As the term progressed, this student wrote papers that were insightful, thought-provoking, and well researched. I was intrigued with Jeffrey Patrick Murray even before our first date.

My vendetta against Catholicism was in full swing. As my philosophy students tackled topics like the meaning of life and the existence of God, I knew that, ideally, instructors are supposed to remain neutral. But I also recalled, from my own college days, how skillfully some professors had dodged this expectation.

There were so many ways to let students know that the professor found certain arguments weak, ineffective, and outdated. A chuckle, a grimace, or a wink and a nod, and many of the arguments seemed to collapse. In my own college days, arguments favoring theism had been dealt with by the professors quickly, as if to suggest they weren't worth spending time on, while proofs against God's existence were presented in scrupulous detail. Now I followed their lead.

I spent plenty of time on one particular argument against God's existence, which traditionally is known as the "problem of evil". God's existence, I explained to my students, isn't possible, since there is suffering in the world. And if God were truly good, he would not allow such suffering to happen. Although our textbook presented many attempts by theists to counteract this claim, I discounted them, one by one.

I was staunchly liberal in all my political opinions, and, like so many professors, I assumed that college was the place to challenge and dismantle traditions. Conservative thought, almost by definition, was the dragon to slay in the classroom, and few students had the courage to disagree with a strongly opinionated professor. Since I was still a fervent feminist, I gave short shrift to moral philosophers who argued in favor of life, and I instead presented the right to abortion as inextricably linked to a woman's ability to live freely. I thought of the fetus as a mere lump of flesh, and since I was still an atheist, I scoffed at viewpoints that said the soul was formed at conception.

"What soul?" I countered. "You can't hear, see, feel, or taste it", I said with disdain, and the same was true of God. I had become a die-hard materialist, and it never occurred to me that the same critique of the soul might be applied to love, honor, peace, and courage.

When the quarter at Georgia Tech was over, Jeffrey Murray and I had lunch together, and soon we discovered we shared much more in common than our interest in philosophy. Like me, he had been raised by a schoolteacher mother and had been overweight as a child. Like me, he had despised tumbling and physical education classes. We both had dabbled in vegetarianism and yoga and were avid readers. He believed in a higher being but had no attachment to any particular religion, although he was fascinated by Eastern thought.

We began dating, although I was extremely skeptical of ever getting seriously involved with a man again. I warned myself, over and over, to keep my emotions from getting out of control and to maintain a safe distance. But here was a man who had not been polluted by the crazy hippie years in Gainesville. He was old-fashioned in the best sense of the word, bringing me chocolates on my birthday and stopping by my office with my favorite ginger cookies. He took me home to meet his family, and I immediately felt at ease: His mother, Lou, encouraged me to eat second helpings, just as my own mother had.

When I went out of town, Jef fed Funky and left cookies in the refrigerator to welcome me home. When I was sick, he came over and made me meals. When I had the blues, which was often, he listened to me and cheered me up. And when, much to my sorrow, Funky's old age caught up with him, Jef carried him to the vet's office and comforted the old boy in his last moments—and then me.

My scrupulous nature had caught up with me, and I was nervous about the thought of giving up entirely on my Ph.D., so I began writing my dissertation and shipping chapters to the professors in Gainesville. The two-hundred-page tome that I went on to produce was liberally peppered with statements about the inequality between men and women, with my proposed solution being androgyny. "It is only by a complete reevaluation of femininity and masculinity that both sexes can be free", I wrote.

Today, this idea strikes me as patently absurd, because I've lived long enough to realize that male-female differences are hard-wired. But back then, I believed that gender differences were the result of conditioning and could be wiped out with new conditioning. In any event, my dissertation, entitled "A Feminist Theory of Authenticity", was accepted, and I returned to Gainesville to get my doctorate in 1981, with Jef and members of my family looking on proudly from the audience.

One evening, while we were eating salads at the Lullwater Tavern near Emory University, Jef mentioned that he would soon be graduating with his master's degree and would be looking for an engineering job, probably out of town. "It would be good if we got married", he said. I had a mouthful of salad and was extremely shocked, although also delighted. Remembering my painful past, though, I answered with a degree of caution: "I'll think about it." He claims that I never really told him yes, but the next time he came over to my apartment, I was looking at dresses in bridal magazines, and he figured that was a good sign.

8

The Empty Nursery

It might seem strange for a woman who billed herself as an atheist to get married in a church, but I felt I had good reasons to choose Druid Hills United Methodist Church in Atlanta. The sanctuary, I told friends, was lovely and would look perfect in the photographs. As for the religious connotations of the ceremony, I figured we could simply ignore them.

The pastor who counseled us before the wedding evidently was not bothered by the bride-to-be's lack of faith or the groom-to-be's stance toward religion, which might be summed up as quasi-pagan-Buddhist-Christian. My future husband professed respect for Christ but saw him merely as another wise and good man, like Buddha. The reverend, a wise man himself, might have glimpsed God's handiwork in our decision to marry in an obviously Christ-centered church, but he didn't say a word.

On June 12, 1982, I decked myself out in a fancy wedding gown, dotted with seed pearls on the bodice, and a veil trimmed in Schiffli lace. Jef's sister, Lisa, read aloud a Shakespearean love sonnet, plus two of our favorite poems by Elizabeth Barrett Browning. The organist that day was

William Krape, and the music, provided by the church musicians, included "The Lord's Prayer" and "The Song of Ruth". I honestly can't recall if we selected those particular pieces or if they were standard fare at all weddings, but in any event, it seems that the Hound of Heaven was slowly making his way into our lives.

Right before the ceremony, something happened that really shook me up. My Aunt Rita, my mother's youngest sister, arrived late and came rushing into the church. When I glanced at her, my heart lurched. The two sisters had always borne a strong resemblance to each other, but this was more than that: I felt that I had glimpsed my own mother's face. I had the strange conviction that, in some inexplicable way, my mother had been present at our wedding, but I kept this mysterious thought tucked away in my heart for years.

We lived in northern Virginia for the first two years of our marriage and then returned to the Atlanta area, where Jef took an engineering job with Hayes Microcomputers. We bought a house in Chelsea Heights in Decatur and settled in with our two cats, Chunky and Snarf. I began teaching English part-time at Mercer University and philosophy at Georgia State, where I continued my fervent campaign to promote atheism.

One of the unspoken rules about success in college is that it is dangerous for students to disagree with the basic values of their instructor. True, there is much lip service given to freedom of expression in the classroom, but in reality, many liberal professors have little patience with solidly conservative students. On many campuses today, for example, premarital sex and same-sex relationships are considered the norm, and students who express criticism of these trends may be ostracized in the classroom.

When I was teaching, I can recall conservative Jewish and Christian students trying to spar with me over the issue of homosexuality, and how I resisted giving credence to the obvious fact that many of the world's religions brand such behavior as unnatural and sinful. Over the years, I have wondered how many of my students might have seriously questioned, or entirely rejected, the faith-based values they brought to college with them and exited my classroom with a thoroughly secular world view. Obviously, there were many students who remained firm in their faith, and I will always remember one named Jill, who shyly gave me a hardbound copy of *Mere Christianity*, by C. S. Lewis.

She wrote inside that she thought I might "like the arguments". I thanked her, although I had no intention of reading a book with that title. But I did keep the book for some reason, and years later, when I read it, I realized that Jill had been doing her own bit of evangelizing.

Once Jef and I were settled in our new house, I began worrying about whether or not to have a child. Most of the women I knew didn't spend time fretting over this decision, but I was a big thinker and prone to analyzing nearly everything. My training in philosophy allowed me to scrutinize both the advantages and disadvantages of a family, while my tendency to worry contributed to an emotional paralysis of sorts.

My husband was mostly neutral and said that if I really wanted a child, we would go ahead. But we also fell into a seesaw dilemma: When I was leaning toward yes, he would start to get nervous and back off, and vice versa. As I fretted, I recalled my mother's dire descriptions of her own pregnancy and how she had nearly died giving birth. Did I want a child badly enough to face a potentially dangerous situation?

"Sometimes at night, struck with an odd, almost queasy, sensation of life slipping away, I think: 'What will it be like to live, and die childless?'" I wrote in my diary. "Then I wonder how I could ever be a mother—the physical strain of pregnancy, the terrible responsibility, the constant chance to turn every moment into an occasion of worry."

Logic seemed to get me nowhere, because I suspected that the apparent disadvantages could be overcome in a flash by parenting's many joys. But I just couldn't do that simple thing that so many people advised, which was following my heart. As a philosopher, I had learned, sadly enough, to distrust the heart when it came to decisions. Everything had to be scrutinized through the lens of reason.

I was growing increasingly frustrated with college teaching and upset that I wasn't giving more energy to writing. Being a writer had been a childhood dream, although majoring in English had somewhat deflated my plans: I had become so awed by the world's great fiction writers that I had concluded it would be hopeless for me even to try. Still, as the years passed, the yearning to write kept niggling at me.

Life seemed agonizingly empty. I was beginning to hate the courses that I was teaching, especially the tedious remedial English courses and logic classes. Although for years I had pined for a full-time teaching job complete with benefits, when a local college offered me just that, I found myself turning down the offer. I simply couldn't stand the thought of grading papers for five sections of English, with thirty students in each section. I suspected that such a prospect would kill any chance of my becoming a writer.

꙳

In my journal, in early 1985, I began expressing a longing for God. I had always been prone to bouts of depression, but now they were particularly debilitating, and I recorded in my diary that I yearned to pray so that I might learn how to accept myself. "Prayer has been so foreign to me", I wrote, and I went on to wonder if I had not lost something inestimably precious when I had turned my back on religion at age nineteen. But this question did not motivate me to rediscover my faith. Instead, I began engaging in a foggy form of prayer directed at an amorphous higher being, which I jokingly called "the goddess".

On February 24, 1985, I wrote in my journal that I had finally reached a decision: I would definitely go ahead and stop using birth control and welcome the chance of pregnancy. I wrote about my yearning to have a little person for whom I could fix Easter baskets and buy Christmas presents, and whom I could love. In the next breath, though, I began worrying again. "I have many doubts about my own physical stamina regarding labor and about parenting itself, an act that seems fraught with mystery", I wrote. Still, I went on to say that I thought we would produce a beautiful child, "mentally, physically, and spiritually".

I decided to have a complete checkup to see if I was in good physical shape for motherhood. But even as I was making the appointment, I began to feel the cold fingers of doubt seizing my heart. I had a tendency toward perfectionism and suspected I would have to give up that inclination, because I knew that a child would bring disorder into my life. I also worried that pregnancy might increase my moodiness and depressive tendencies. As the demons of doubt rushed in, I tried to forestall them with my dreams of how I would raise the child to be different than I was. The child would be confident and secure, not tortured by anxiety and indecision as I was.

Ironically, the doctor I went to see turned out to be exactly my age, thirty-seven—and pregnant. She was confident and enthusiastic and assured me that there was nothing physical standing in the way of motherhood for me. Back at home, I started establishing new goals: I would lose ten pounds immediately, so that if I gained twenty-five pounds during pregnancy, I wouldn't be too heavy after the birth.

Six months passed, and the "baby issue", as I called it, was still a huge torment for me. I simply could not do what other women were doing, which was "letting go and letting God", because I didn't believe in God. Every time I considered giving up birth control, an odd terror seized me. Caught in an obsessive web of worry, I began to see the first in a series of therapists, with the intention of resolving this issue before I was too old.

On December 2, 1985, I had a conversation with my Aunt Rita that seemed very telling. After listening to me lament over my inability to make a decision, she said simply, "Lorraine, if you had wanted to have a baby, you would have had one by now." She also said, "I think you can live a rich, satisfying life without children." Two months later, I wrote in my journal that I was starting to believe that if I closed the door on motherhood, other doors might open, "adventures not yet dreamed of!"

Feminists of the day had written numerous books and articles touting what was called a "child-free" life. They asserted that using the term "childless" was wrong, because it sounded pejorative, and living without children was actually a wonderful, freeing experience. In an odd twist of logic, these child-free advocates celebrated the empty nursery as a sign of liberation. After all, without children, you could travel, sleep in on weekends, and have more money in the bank. Since I was deeply ambivalent about motherhood, I jumped on board the child-free bandwagon. It didn't occur to me that the position was inherently flawed, because if everyone gave up having children, the human race would die out.

I also didn't see the fundamental disconnect in feminism: Although feminists were supposed to celebrate women's choices, they roundly denigrated traditional paths like marriage and family. At the very least, feminists insisted, a family should be postponed until a woman had reached her career goals. And, of course, if a pregnancy occurred at an inconvenient time, the backup birth control method was abortion.

The secular mind-set that pervaded feminism dictated what was important: education, jobs, salaries, and promotions. Family and other human relationships were relegated to the backseat. As in the story about the emperor's new clothes, it seemed that no one had the courage to declare the obvious: The voluntarily childless path is woefully selfish. For one, the decision does not just affect the couple alone. In our case, Jef's siblings never had a chance to experience being an aunt or uncle, and his mother never became a grandmother. My sister never knew the joys of being an aunt, and her children had no maternal cousins. If it takes a village—or at least aunts, uncles, and grandparents—to help rear a child, then it seems obvious that abstaining from parenthood harms that same village.

❦

By July 1986 my fretting over motherhood was in full swing again, and I once more began seeing a therapist. He advised me, even though I was nearly thirty-nine years old, to take my time with the issue that he called the "biological clock". As the new year dawned in 1988, I was still discussing the question about children with the same therapist, even though I was then over forty years old! It may seem extremely odd that he was still accepting my money, but he subscribed to a popular theory that said it was fine to postpone motherhood until women were well into their forties.

I went to three different therapists as I agonized over my decision. The first two remained neutral and simply listened to my endless lists of "on the one hand" and "on the other hand". But the third one, listening to my stories about my past and the painful things that had happened, said something that really shocked me. She never used the words "absolution" and "confession", but she did say, finally, that she didn't think she could help me. She believed that I needed spiritual help. I was shocked by her comment and didn't realize that, in a few years, she would be proven right.

Despite the criticisms many people make about the Catholic Church's opposition to artificial birth control, I would say that, for ambivalent women like me, access to contraceptive devices and pills can contribute to emotional paralysis. A generation ago, I would not have had time or money to waste in therapists' offices, hashing over the pros and cons of child rearing. Instead, nature probably would have taken its course, and I might have been too busy feeding, diapering, and loving babies.

9

Twitches upon the Thread

I was certainly the poster child for ambivalence over motherhood, but I never waffled about my goal of becoming a published writer. In December 1985, with help from my brother-in-law Steve Murray, an accomplished journalist, I had begun free-lancing for an independent Atlanta newspaper. From the day I arose before dawn to drive to the nearest newsstand to pick up a copy of *Southline* newspaper, with my feature story prominently displayed on the front page, I was hooked.

Paul was a perfect editor. Over coffee, we discussed different angles for my story ideas, and he recommended articles and books for me to read. He was well versed on philosophical, historical, and political topics, but one day I discovered something about this brilliant man that both repelled and intrigued me. He was a Catholic!

I had admired the intellects of so many atheists in my college years and had so strongly associated Catholicism with my antiquated childhood beliefs that I had arrived at the ridiculous, deeply arrogant conclusion that Catholics couldn't possibly be bright. The one who wasn't bright, though, was none other than me. Despite my advanced degrees in philosophy and English, I had never read the works of

Thomas Aquinas or Augustine, nor had I encountered more contemporary figures like J. R. R. Tolkien and G. K. Chesterton, strong defenders of the Catholic faith. I had read fictional works by Flannery O'Connor and Walker Percy in college, but my professors had presented their Catholicism as more of an aberration than an integral feature of their art.

G. K. Chesterton compares God's action in the conversion experience to an "unseen hook and an invisible line which is long enough to let [a man] wander to the ends of the world, and still to bring him back with a twitch upon the thread".[1] Looking back, I can see evidence that God was gently twitching my thread as I began writing for *Southline*. Many of the story ideas that came to me "out of the blue", as I was waking up in the morning, were decidedly religious in nature. Inspiration, I would later realize, was something that reason couldn't easily put into a neat little box.

As a result of my early-morning musings, I found myself writing features about cloistered nuns who lived at the Monastery of the Visitation in a nearby town and about Protestant women who become ministers. With Paul's cheerful approval, I also wrote an article in October 1986 that explored various definitions of sin, including Jewish, Baptist, Buddhist— and, oh yes, Catholic.

I couldn't resist expressing my own anti-Catholic leanings in my writing. In the article about Atlanta clergywomen, for example, I poked fun at myself for the days when I used to say the Rosary. Writing about sin, I mentioned my fear of interviewing a "wizened priest in black robes, a vestige of my schoolgirl days, who will somehow peer into my soul and tally up the black marks with horror". In that particular story, though, I did go on to say that Father Dominic Young, the teacher I interviewed from Saint Pius X Catholic High School, put me at ease immediately. In my typically arrogant way, I concluded from his insightful statements that the Church had "come a long way" since my childhood.

Asked about sin, Father Young explained that Catholicism sees human beings as created freely and lovingly by God. We are, however, born into a fallen world, which is the result of Adam and Eve turning their backs on God. He defined sin as the process of rejecting God's love and mentioned that the healing process for sinners begins with the sacrament of confession. Despite the obvious suitability of his words to my life experiences, it never dawned on me that his comments might have been "a twitch upon the thread".

I concluded the article with his quote: "Man cannot be satisfied with material goods. There has to be spiritual integrity." A few months later, I heard the same words echoed at the cloistered monastery, as the nuns shyly told me about their journeys into religious life. I remember being somewhat mystified when one of the younger nuns told me that she had been ironing a favorite dress for a party and accidentally burned it. In that moment, she realized that "nothing material ever satisfies."

As for me, it would take more than a burned dress to convince me of the futility of materialism. My main cure for the blues was heading to the mall and coming home with new dresses, shoes, sweaters, and trinkets. Although I never fell seriously into debt, I rarely had any savings to speak of because I couldn't seem to get enough new stuff. My bouts of depression continued, even though I was happily married and had a home, a teaching job, and the chance to do free-lance writing. Was it possible there was something more to life?

❧

God continued working gently behind the scenes. One day, Jef and I found a large white cockatoo sitting beneath the bird feeder in our front yard. When Jef retrieved him, he discovered the bird was tame, and we took him inside and made him our pet. The first time I went to stroke the bird's head, he bowed to me, and I remember thinking that his wings reminded me in some way of an angel, a word that meant "messenger". I didn't tell my husband about my strange impression of the bird, but shortly after, he suggested we call the animal Pooks, short for "Pookah", which means "spirit".

Another time, we found an orphaned baby squirrel in our yard, and we went on to raise it to fuzzy adulthood. I then began volunteering as an animal rehabilitator and took in numerous baby squirrels over the next few years. These tiny creatures, which came to me furless and with eyes still shut, had never seen their mothers but still knew exactly what to do the first time I gave them pecans: They rolled the nut around in their paws to test for soundness, and if the nut passed the test, they buried it for later consumption. The little ones also needed no instruction from me in the art of building a fine nest. Face to face with the mystery of instinct, I didn't realize that I was witnessing the imprint of the Creator.

In 1989, I decided that if I had to draw one more Venn diagram on the blackboard or explain to another student the definition of a sentence fragment, I would go mad. I said good-bye to college teaching and began working as a writer in the publications office of Kennesaw State College, thirty miles north of our home. My boss was a big-hearted Southern lady with a down-home sense of humor. One day, in a casual conversation, she mentioned going to church to worship with her family, and I thought she was joking. Later, I realized that she was a devout Christian and quite active in her church. Puzzling over her remark about worship for quite a while, I found it strange and unsettling. I wondered: Did people still do that kind of thing?

Jef began working at the Georgia Tech Research Institute, and between the two of us, we were making a good amount of money. Since we loved vacationing on the island of Cedar Key, Florida, we decided to build a vacation home, with the goal of relocating there in the future. As the new year dawned in 1991, we spent our first night in the house that we called the Marsh Nest, celebrating with champagne and stone-crab claws.

About a year later, our lives started going through some radical changes. Jef returned from a business trip to New York City and casually announced that he had stopped in at Saint Patrick's Cathedral, where he had lit votive candles in memory of his dad and my parents. Somehow, the remark hit me hard. I wondered, what would have prompted someone who knew very little about the Catholic tradition of lighting candles for the dead, to do exactly that?

It didn't take me long to realize that I had failed in my responsibility to my parents, at least according to the Catholic beliefs of my childhood. I had neither prayed for the repose of their souls nor had Masses said in their behalf. Remembering myself as the little girl who had nearly worn the veneer off her beads as she prayed for the poor souls in Purgatory, I felt a sense of loss. What had happened to her?

About the same time, I noticed a book that had been sitting unnoticed on our shelves for many years. I couldn't recall buying it, but now it seemed to light up and shout, "Read me!" It was Thomas Merton's *Seven Storey Mountain*, which was touted on the back cover as "one of the most famous books ever written on a man's search for faith and peace".

On a whim, I plopped down on the couch and began reading. As I turned the pages, I began to get an uneasy feeling, as if some inexplicable, nameless force was moving through my life like a current, slowly sweeping me toward an unknown destination. Merton's journey impressed itself deeply on me. Raised a Christian, he had wandered far from the fold and, like me, led an extremely decadent life in his twenties. Eventually, he converted to Catholicism and then entered a monastery. I wondered: Why in the world did his story hold me in such thrall?

I was unaware that C. S. Lewis, a former atheist who had converted to Christianity, had written: "A young man who wishes to remain a sound Atheist cannot be too careful of his reading." [2] This observation turned out to be right on target in my case, especially when I discovered one passage in Merton's book that particularly impressed me, given my reaction to my boss' comment about worshipping: "One came out of the church with a kind of comfortable and satisfied feeling that something had been done that needed to be done." [3]

"It is a law of man's nature, written into his very essence," Merton wrote, "and just as much a part of him as the desire to build houses and cultivate the land and marry and have children and read books and sing songs, that he should want to stand together with other men ... to acknowledge their common dependence on God, their Father and Creator." [4]

This passage occurred early in the narrative, and the mystery is that I did not laugh and throw the book down. Years later, I would discover that C. S. Lewis had been strongly influenced by the writings of another convert, G. K. Chesterton. Lewis suggested that Providence "quite overrules our previous tastes when it decides to bring two minds together" and said that liking an author may be as involuntary and improbable as falling in love.[5] Oddly enough, it seems that I was falling in love with Thomas Merton, a monk who had died in 1968, during my wild escapades in Gainesville.

Cedar Key continued to captivate us, and we escaped to our Marsh Nest whenever we could. In our small, no-frills boat, which we christened the Sea Moose, we roamed around the barrier islands and were mesmerized by the abundance of birds and fish that called the islands home. For the first time in my life, I became attuned to the predictability of the rising and falling tides and began to wonder about the precision underpinning the workings of nature.

On one boating trip, we were greeted by an eager crowd of almost two hundred pelicans, which surrounded us when we began doling out cigar minnows. In the presence of this elaborate cast of characters, I found myself thinking about the existence of the author who had shaped it. I was, of course, familiar with the standard proofs and refutations for God's existence, but real-life boating in Cedar Key trumped the cut-and-dried logical categories in philosophy books.

They say there are no atheists in foxholes, but on a pitch-black night, when we rode the Sea Moose through a rocky and stormy sea, I concluded that there are few nonbelievers in small boats. Why was it that I found myself praying during that terrifying journey? Was it just an old habit? But there were other old habits that I had given up, like knocking on wood and carrying a rabbit's foot. Why did this habit comfort me and seem just right during that storm, when I was really scared? I thought about the little squirrels and how they know how to build nests without anyone teaching them, and I began to wonder if Merton was right. Was it possible that some impulses, like the desire to love—and pray—had been imbedded in the human heart by a higher being?

On July 4, 1993, Jef and I had dropped anchor and were eating our lunch near Piney Point, a cove in Cedar Key. We were enjoying the glassy swell of the gulf and the clean stretch of aqua sky, laced with threads of clouds, when we suddenly heard a loud splash just a few feet away. The still waters parted, and up popped the heads of two enormous creatures.

I was so stunned that I could not find the word to match the image until the twosome disappeared beneath the water. "Manatees!" I shouted, and we burst into delighted laughter. Moments later, the creatures again lifted their heads from the water, peered into the boat, and then, as quickly as they had appeared, swam away. The atheist in the boat, stunned by their eyes, which seemed so deeply innocent and mysterious, now uttered a rather strange statement: "It was like looking into the face of God!"

Later, I wrote in my journal: "When I was a child, much was made of the Beatific Vision, that moment in heaven when we will finally look into the eyes of God. I am starting to believe we have glimpses of God's face here on earth. And I believe we had a glimpse at Piney Point. That deep spark of recognition, topped with wonder, joy, laughter, absolute delight! The manatees changed my world view forever."

By day, red-winged blackbirds and grackles produced a raucous symphony on Cedar Key, punctuated by the occasional squawks of blue herons, while at night, frogs, cicadas, and crickets took up the slack. At times, I had the eerie sense that they were all part of some choir, raising their voices in praise of their Creator. "The gulf itself seems part of God's breath", I wrote in my journal, as I gradually became more and more comfortable using the "G" word. "He inhales, the tides recede, and the mudflats are stripped, revealing cities of oysters, fiddler crabs, and whelks. He exhales, and the tides rush back."

Years later, when I discovered that Thomas à Kempis had suggested that "every creature [can] be a mirror of life and a book of heavenly teaching",[6] I concluded that the island of Cedar Key was overflowing with celestial books.

Chinks in My Feminist Armor

The twitch on my line seemed to be growing stronger and more insistent. One Saturday night, we were sitting on our deck in Decatur, eating a sumptuous array of appetizers, when suddenly the image of a nearby church flashed into my mind. "Let's walk over and take a look", I said, and Jef was open to the suggestion.

On that first visit to Saint Thomas More Catholic Church, we merely glanced inside, admired the stained-glass windows, and picked up a bulletin. But later that night, as the lightning bugs pierced the blackness, we lit candles on the deck and talked in depth about our childhood beliefs about God and religion. It was then that I first told my husband about my perplexing feeling that "someone" was calling me.

It also seemed that this someone was sending messages from various ports. It wasn't just the encounter with the manatees, it wasn't just the event at Saint Patrick's Cathedral, and it wasn't simply Thomas Merton's book. The messages seemed imbedded in all these events, which were prodding me to dig deeper into this mystery.

A week later, we walked to the church on Sunday morning and stood in the vestibule because we were too hesitant actually to sit in a pew. The priest celebrating Mass that day was Father Patrick Mulhern, whose sermon drew together so many different threads of human experience, with snippets taken from a variety of writers and philosophers, that I was stunned.

I suppose I'd expected him to sound like the priests from my childhood, in the days when most sermons had gone right over my head. But this priest was talking about real-life things, the pain and worry of daily life, the moments when God seems far away, and the times we question why we have to suffer. I turned to Jef and whispered what was for me the ultimate compliment: "He sounds like a Buddhist!"

After more candlelit discussions on the deck, we decided to take the next step. Jef was interested in learning more about Catholicism, while I wanted to explore more deeply exactly where my yearnings were coming from. Thomas Merton's book had introduced me to a man with a keen intellect, a vast amount of education, and a zeal for passionate living. That this man had followed his heart on a journey that led to Catholicism, which he saw as the most complete form of Christianity, definitely intrigued me.

After making an appointment, we went to the rectory one evening to talk with Father Byron, another priest at Saint Thomas More at the time. Father Byron was a clergyman from the old school, and Father Mulhern was not, although we didn't realize this distinction then.

Father Byron, a rather old, wizened man with thinning white hair, cordially welcomed us to the rectory and then talked with us individually. When it was my turn and he realized how long I had been away from the Church, and how many years I had been married, this old-fashioned priest cut to the chase. He asked me straight out if I was doing anything to prevent the conception of children. I was shocked, astonished, aghast, mortified, and furious.

I can't recall how I answered, but I managed to control my emotions. When we left the rectory, however, my voice was trembling with anger as I told Jef what had happened. I passionately emphasized that he could do whatever he wanted, but I would have nothing more to do with Catholicism, ever. A few days later, though, after my temper had cooled down a bit, I found myself picking up the phone and calling Paul, my Catholic friend and editor.

I guess I wanted to figure out if all Catholics were like Father Byron, and I had made up my mind that if Paul took Father's side, then I would go no further with my search. Paul, however, reacted with indignation about what had happened and he advised me to call the pastor.

Father Patrick Mulhern found my story rather zany, maybe because he was well aware of the other priest's strict leanings and had probably heard these tales before. He invited us to return to the rectory for another visit. When we did, he came bustling happily out and welcomed me with a hug. This was the gesture that I had yearned for: Someone to accept me as I was then, rather than demanding that I become the perfect Catholic at a moment's notice.

Father Pat was a tall, middle-aged man with sea-blue eyes and sharp cheekbones. As I told him a little about my spiritual journey and my suspicion that I was being pulled, slowly but surely, back to the Church, he nodded and listened intently. But I also apologized to him, because I felt like a bit of an imposter, since my faith was only the size of a "tiny seed". I didn't realize that I was echoing Christ's parable about the mustard seed, but surely this seasoned priest did, and he assured me that the small seed would grow. When he invited me into the church, I remembered my childhood belief in the Real Presence of Christ in the Eucharist and in the tabernacle, and I automatically genuflected out of respect.

The Real Presence, I remembered, was one of the beliefs that made Catholicism unique and had been a cornerstone of Christianity for over fifteen hundred years before being rejected by Protestants after the Reformation. I began to suspect at that moment why my search was taking me to the Catholic Church: It was the divine presence on earth that I was seeking, and God's true presence in the Eucharist.

As I knelt down, I recalled the story about the Good Shepherd, who goes after the sheep that strays. The story never said why the sheep had left the fold, but that night, I wondered if perhaps, like me, it had been a rebel. With that image in mind, for the first time in over twenty years, I uttered a very simple prayer to the One on the altar: "Help me to believe."

As the months wore on, I became more convinced that, despite my many disagreements with Church teachings on social issues, my journey was taking me back to Catholicism. True, I wasn't returning in a wholehearted way, since I still believed that abortion and euthanasia were justified in certain circumstances. I also thought women should be able to be ordained and that priests should be allowed to marry. There were obviously Protestant denominations where these points would not be obstacles, but the Hound of Heaven had nudged me into a Catholic church, and I would not argue.

In truth, despite my years in Catholic schools, I was woefully ignorant of the background and history of Church teachings and thought my opinions were just as valid as those of the saints and Fathers of the Church. Once again, arrogance seemed to be my "sin du jour". Still, it seems that God was calling me back in my brokenness, with all my disagreements and provisos, and evidently was willing to let my conversion be a work in progress. As Flannery O'Connor so aptly put it, "I think most people come to the [Catholic] Church by means the Church does not allow. . . ." She went on to say, "The Church is entirely set up for the sinner; which creates much misunderstanding among the smug." [1]

When Jef expressed his interest in learning about Catholic teachings, Father Pat gave him a book to read and said he would be happy to answer questions. We were both impressed with the priest's subtle, nonaggressive approach. He was clearly not going to try to "sell" religion to us but rather seemed to trust that things would work out in God's time.

Jef and I snuggled up on the couch as we usually did in the evenings, and he began reading the book while I did something I had avoided for years, which was picking up the Bible and reading the Gospels. As I turned the pages, I was surprised at the person whom I encountered there. This Jesus seemed so compelling, so kind—and so wise. I was all too familiar with Western philosophers, spanning the gamut from Plato and Aristotle to Kierkegaard and Husserl, but their wisdom now seemed feeble in comparison. As C. S. Lewis so aptly put it, Christ in the Gospels is "lit by a light from beyond the world". [2]

I was especially moved by the passage that occurs before the Crucifixion, when Jesus is standing before Pilate and says that he came into the world "to testify to the truth". Pilate's famous reply is, "What is truth?" (Jn 18:38). In that moment, I felt exactly like Pilate. I had spent so many years as a philosopher, analyzing everything to death and getting nowhere, and, like Pilate, I had been blind to the God who had been standing right in front of me. At the start of this particular journey, I had told my husband that I wanted to figure out where my yearnings were coming from. As I read the Gospels, I had no doubt that they were coming from Christ.

❧

We began going to Mass on Sundays, and each week the Gospel readings impressed me deeply. I also loved the prayers during Mass, and the way the liturgy opened with "The grace of our Lord Jesus Christ and the love of God and the fellowship of the Holy Spirit be with you all." I was moved by the humble words that preceded Communion: "Lord, I am not worthy to receive you, but only say the word, and I shall be healed."

Another scene in the Gospels especially touched me, because I so strongly identified with the events. In the story, Jesus is having supper at the home of a Pharisee when a woman suddenly bursts into the house. The host is horrified because the woman is a known sinner, and Jesus is well aware of her reputation too. Still, Jesus doesn't shrink when she bathes the dust from his feet with her tears and dries his feet with her hair. Aware of the host's disapproval, Jesus explains that the woman's sins have been forgiven because of her act of love.

I thought about all the years when I had sought comfort in the arms of the wrong men, all the sins I had committed, and all the times I had wept. Surely I had produced enough tears to wash Jesus' feet as well. I had to wonder: How had I managed to miss the love and mercy that Jesus expressed, over and over, in the Gospels? Why had I made fun of people who went to church? Why had I mocked Christians, in the days when a good Jesus joke would bring a hearty laugh from my friends?

A passage from Thomas Merton, written about his life when he was eighteen, seemed to describe the old me: "I was stamping the last remains of spiritual vitality out of my own soul, and trying with all my might to crush and obliterate the image of the divine liberty that had been implanted in me by God." Merton added that he had, unknowingly, been participating in Christ's agony: "This is the crucifixion of Christ: in which He dies again and again in the individuals who were made to share the joy and freedom of His grace, and who deny Him." [3] Somehow, when I looked back on my life, I could see myself standing at the foot of the Cross, helping to pound in the nails.

I began to revisit the anger toward God that had festered in me since my mother's death. Why had I blamed God and believed that he had willfully deprived me of her when many people, like Merton, lose their mothers when they are children? My own husband had lost his father at the age of six, yet he had not harbored a grudge against God. It was true that, from my perspective, my mother had not lived long enough, but she was with me until I was twenty-nine. I began to understand that, for people who believe in the promises of Christ, physical death was a stepping stone to something more. I also began to wonder if someday I might meet my mother again, under very different circumstances.

One day, I stumbled upon a book about Mother Teresa, and I was impressed by her selfless devotion to the poor.

Still, when I read about her advocacy for the Catholic pro-life contingent, my demon of arrogance reared its ugly head again. "Yes, she is a saintly woman," I thought, "but terribly out of step with modern times!"

As a feminist, I found Church teachings on abortion to be flat-out antiquated and ridiculous. This was the twentieth century, after all, and a woman had a right to do whatever she wanted with her own body! It never occurred to me that our bodies—and our lives—were really gifts from God. I couldn't see how "me-centered" the typical feminist stance was: A woman's body, career, and goals were supposed to come before anyone else, even a helpless baby in the womb. But there was a deeper reason that I clung so ardently to my beliefs. Years ago, when a pregnancy test had come back positive, I had walked into a feminist clinic and availed myself of a modern woman's legal right to an abortion.

My fierce adherence to the feminist stance on abortion was part and parcel of my anti-Catholic vendetta: If the Church was opposed to X, then it was likely why I would be in favor of it. As a philosophy teacher, I had examined the moral issue of abortion and had decided that a woman's rights always took precedence over the amorphous entity known as the "fetus". And so, when I became pregnant but was unmarried, I didn't stop to debate the morality of what I should do, since my mind was already made up. Having read numerous journal articles that made abortion sound as simple and straightforward as a dental procedure, I concluded it would be a quick and efficient way to solve the problem.

I went into the clinic expecting a relatively pain-free experience, but I came out feeling that the authors of these articles had betrayed me. The procedure was agonizing, since no pain relievers were offered. That shocking experience was the first chink in the armor of feminism that I wore. Still, despite the pain, I did leave the clinic feeling very relieved: My problem was solved, and I could return to life as usual.

No one, however, had prepared me for the flashbacks, which began about a year after the "procedure", as I thought of it. Each time, I would relive the experience: going into the clinic; getting up on the table; experiencing the searing, unbelievable pain; and then lying there, gasping and stunned. Each time, I would squeeze the hand of the woman standing beside me, a volunteer who was there to offer compassion and who surely thought she was doing the right thing.

I started having upsetting reactions to babies. I would be walking around in a grocery store, and if I spotted an infant, my eyes would fill with stinging tears and I would walk quickly away. A question started plaguing me: How old would my baby have been now?

❦

In the fall of 1993, Jef enrolled in a program at Saint Thomas More designed for people who wanted to learn more about Catholicism. It was called the Rite of Christian Initiation for Adults and met on Thursday evenings. I often went with him to the meetings because I was hungry to know more about the faith that I had left behind. We became friends with people in the group, and I will always remember a little Italian lady named Rosa, a volunteer who brought refreshments and whom I thought of as "the Cookie Lady".

I was astonished that the whole program was run by volunteers, who evidently considered their time well spent in helping other people on their faith journeys. I also was surprised at how many other church activities, whether it was running the nursery school, preparing dinners, or helping at homeless shelters, were done by volunteers. I recalled the catechism answer from so long ago that said that God had created us to know, love, and serve him. It seemed that these people, acting out of love to serve others, had found life's meaning.

My memories about the abortion continued to haunt me. Even though I remained staunchly pro-choice, I still had to battle a deep and gnawing sense that I had done something terribly wrong. After all, I could have given the child up for adoption, but I had instead chosen what I thought was the simpler route. And although I agreed with those who said abortion was just a medical procedure and a woman's legal right, my heart was hinting that it was something else.

Jef told me about an Advent penance service to be held at the church on December 15, 1993. I had not been to confession for many years and dreaded the prospect, and on that bleak, frigid night, I had also fallen into one of my frequent blue moods and didn't want to budge from the couch. But after he assured me repeatedly that I would feel better if I went, I put on my coat and climbed, resentfully and reluctantly, into the car.

In *Surprised by Joy*, C. S. Lewis said he had been stalked for years by the steady, unrelenting approach of "Him who I so earnestly desired not to meet".[4] When Lewis finally began praying, he was stunned by the humility of a God who will accept even the most reluctant converts. "The Prodigal Son at least walked home on his own feet", wrote Lewis. "But who can duly adore that Love which will open the high gates to a prodigal who is brought in kicking, struggling, resentful, and darting his eyes in every direction for a chance of escape?"[5]

As I entered the crowded church that night, where six priests were hearing confessions, I felt like that resentful and struggling prodigal. And as I huddled in line, wrapped miserably in my heavy coat, I remembered the counselor I had seen years ago who had hinted that what I needed was spiritual absolution. Here was my chance, but my heart was throbbing wildly, and I was tempted to turn and run away.

The line inched forward, and soon it was my turn. The confessional was situated in a small room behind the altar, where one could either kneel behind a privacy screen or take a chair and face the priest. I huddled behind the screen. My fear was that the priest would not give me absolution. Worse yet, he would be so outraged at what I had done that he would yell at me. He might even tell me there was no way I could ever come back to the Catholic Church, given the severity of my sins. The people in line would hear him shouting at me, and then I would have to walk back out while they stared at me, wondering what hideous, unforgivable sin this poor woman had committed.

II

Farewell to the Little Soul

There was no escape, so I knelt down and whispered the words that the sisters had taught me long ago: "Bless me, Father, for I have sinned." Then, with tears streaming down my cheeks, I told him about the abortion.

As I wept, the priest remained calm. He expressed neither horror nor anger. When I had finally composed myself long enough to say that I could not forgive myself, he quietly asked me if I thought God would forgive me. When I said that I didn't know, he reminded me of the parable of the prodigal son: The son returns to the father, as I was doing, only because he implicitly believes that he will be forgiven.

In a heavy accent that I think was African, the priest, whose name I believe was Father Joseph, went on to say something that surprised me. He said he was so happy that God had given me the grace to return to the Church. To underscore Christ's mercy and forgiveness, he told me the story about the two thieves who died beside Jesus and how Jesus turned to one and said, "Today you will be with me in Paradise" (Lk 23:43).

Father Joseph explained that the people who had crucified Jesus had been ignorant of who he really was. He compared their ignorance to my not understanding the full implications of what I had done that day in the abortion clinic. He reminded me that Jesus had said, "Father, forgive them; for they know not what they do" (Lk 23:34). Father Joseph assured me that Jesus would forgive me too.

Through my tears, I asked him the question that had gnawed at my heart for years. "Father, what happened to that little soul?" He didn't hesitate: "God takes care of the little souls." How I had longed to hear these words! Now I didn't have to worry anymore. God would embrace that innocent little being, who never had a chance to take a first breath. After divulging my other sins, I left the confessional, and I remembered what Sister had said so long ago about God's merciful grace washing over my soul. I felt that I was free. The rope binding me to my painful past had been severed.

During Mass one Sunday, Father Pat introduced four diminutive sisters to the congregation: "These are the Missionaries of Charity, who have been sent by Mother Teresa to Atlanta to open a home for women with AIDS." The moment the foursome shyly stood up, dressed in white saris with blue stripes along the edges, a thought flashed into my mind: "This is it! This is what I have been looking for!"

Ever since I had heard the Gospel reading in which Christ had described himself as the one who had "come not to be served but to serve", I had been searching for a way to help others. Now I couldn't wait for Mass to be over, so we could meet these sisters. When we introduced ourselves to them, I asked the nun in charge, Sister Reggie Paul, if we could help them in any way. With a very big smile, Sister assured us that the sisters needed plenty of help getting the house ready to become a home.

Nearly every Saturday for the next year, Jef and I rose early, made a thermos of coffee, donned our work clothes, packed tools, and headed over to the dilapidated house on Saint Charles Avenue. During the week, we often went to 7 A.M. Mass in the sisters' small, humble chapel, where there were always a few flowers, simply arranged in a vase on the altar.

Everything was simple in their world. The chapel had a hand-printed sign near the crucifix, with the words of Jesus, spoken from the Cross, words that appeared in the Missionaries of Charity chapels all over the world: "I thirst." The sisters dedicated their lives to quenching Jesus' thirst for love. They lived according to a strict regimen, arising before dawn every day and attending Mass and then spending much of the day ministering to others and praying. Their humble routine centered on ordinary things like washing clothes and cooking but always included praying, reading Scripture, and receiving Communion.

As the months wore on, we became very close with the sisters and often joined them for the Rosary in the afternoons. They chanted the prayers in a precise way, each side of the room taking turns, and with the voices blending into one. The result was the gradual lessening of my usual mental chatter. Then there was a long period of complete silence, broken only by the sounds of birdsong and the occasional tooting of a car horn. I couldn't help but remember my days in the Buddhist meditation center, when I had struggled in silence with my painful thoughts, but there was one huge difference: In this chapel, we were in the presence of Christ in the tabernacle.

One day, during Mass in their tiny chapel, where everyone sat on the floor, as in India, Father John Fallon said something in his sermon that stunned me: "Some people think Jesus came for the saints or for Mother Teresa but not for them." I realized in that moment that I was one of these people. I could see that Christ would love the sisters and would cherish my husband, but the notion that he might actually love me was very hard to grasp. After all, I had been the child who had followed her own mother around, asking, "Do you love me?" I had been the one whose father had been so withdrawn and who had endured so many relationships with Mr. Wrong. No wonder that God's love seemed elusive to me.

In the old house on Saint Charles Avenue, a crew of volunteers showed their love for the sisters by helping them scrape paint off creaky cabinets and refinish floors. We painted, we scrubbed, and we hammered. The volunteers, all ages, sizes, shapes, colors, and religions, came from all over Atlanta to get the house ready. It took more than a year of hard work on the part of many people before the house was in decent enough shape to open officially. When I first heard that it would be called the Gift of Grace, I immediately thought about my mother.

The sisters helped deepen my faith. They seemed childlike in many ways and humble, yet because of their solid faith and prayer life, they were capable of tending to terminally ill people, whom many others couldn't bear to be around. They were familiar with death and had sat at the bedsides of countless women who were in the throes of dying from AIDS and other diseases. In this way, they had great wisdom. They rarely used the word "I" and never asked for things for themselves, with one exception. They were never shy about asking for prayers.

The nuns lived as poor people do, with just the bare necessities, but they always seemed joyful, maybe because they had access to a spiritual array of riches: daily Mass, the Liturgy of the Hours prayed throughout the day, and silent adoration of Jesus in the Eucharist during afternoons in the chapel.

The humble sisters provided the ailing women, many of whom had lived in dire poverty on the streets of Atlanta, with their first safe home and the first experience of being cared for. The nuns were the perfect example of women whose entire existences revolved around that simple catechism answer I had memorized so long ago. They strived to know God through hearing the Gospels, receiving daily Communion, and spending time with him in prayer. They went on to serve and love him by taking care of the women.

One of the inspirations for Mother Teresa's ministry to the poorest of the poor was the scriptural passage in Matthew 25 in which Jesus told his disciples to look for him in the hungry, the homeless, and the imprisoned. The disciples were baffled at first, when Christ said, "For I was hungry and you gave me food" and "I was in prison and you visited me." When, they wondered, had they ever done these things? But when Christ said, "Whatever you did for one of these least brothers of mine, you did for me", that was the message that set the fire of love burning in Mother Teresa's heart. In a mystical way, she emphasized that when her nuns ministered to the world's dying and poor people, they were taking care of Jesus.

The nuns were the furthest thing from self-centered and the last people in the world to defend their rights or to assert themselves. In my days as an ardent feminist, I would have scoffed at how meek and unselfassuming they were. They weren't concerned about goals, accomplishments, or applause. They simply did what needed to be done and got up the next day to do it over again.

They scrubbed floors, peeled carrots, bathed their patients, and hung clothes on the line. Most of all, they tried to radiate the love of Christ to women who had been the castoffs of society. I recalled how Simone de Beauvoir had railed against the menial tasks that women do because the tasks are so repetitious and seem to produce nothing lasting. I realized with a bit of a shock that the sisters were very much like housewives, performing humble and repetitive tasks.

Yes, it might be true that the work they did one day had to be repeated the next, but from the Christian point of view, the nuns—just like mothers—were caring for people with immortal souls. No work could be more important. As Alice von Hildebrand put it in *The Privilege of Being a Woman*, "One day, all human accomplishments will be reduced to a pile of ashes. But every single child to whom a woman has given birth will last forever, for he has been given an immortal soul made to God's image and likeness." [1]

Up till now, Jef and I had done no real community service. Instead, we had enjoyed our free time on the weekends, puttering around and doing whatever we wanted to do. Now we found ourselves coming home with aching muscles after long hours spent working side by side with the volunteers and the sisters. We felt tired but also oddly happy, because for the first time in our married life together, we were part of something bigger than ourselves.

Unfortunately, a few months after going to confession, my fretting and self-recrimination about the abortion began anew.

I believed that God had forgiven me, but being merciful to myself evidently was going to be much harder. One day I spotted an ad in our church bulletin for a pro bono group called PATH (Post-Abortion Treatment and Healing). Without hesitating, I called the number and spoke with a woman with a sweet and gentle voice who said she would come to my church and meet me.

A few nights later, Mary Ann met me in the sanctuary, where we sat alone, talking quietly in the choir area. Through a deluge of tears, I told her my story and confessed that I was still struggling to forgive myself. As I wept, her eyes filled with tears too. She assured me that my feelings were normal and that, like many other women, I needed more time to heal emotionally. She suggested a path to healing that would come about through discussing a book called *Forgiven and Set Free.*

The book contained passages from Scripture to remind women who had been through abortions about the reality of God's mercy and forgiveness. As the months passed, my sessions with Mary Ann helped me gradually to heal. It was a great comfort to have another woman to confide in about that day long ago, and I felt that God had sent me Mary Ann to help me. Years later, I would read these words in *The Privilege of Being a Woman* and think of her: "Those who devote their loving attention to [women who have had abortions] know that the wound created in their souls is so deep that only God's grace can heal it." [2]

In their chapel, the sisters had a blackboard on which they would write the names of people who needed special prayers. On the morning of February 14, 1994, the blackboard read:

"Pray for Lorraine and Jef." We would be getting married sacramentally and officially in the Catholic Church later that day.

We were learning something about the Church that many outsiders might find very perplexing. Legally, of course, we were married in the eyes of the state, but canon law said that a baptized Catholic like myself had to receive the sacrament of marriage in the Catholic Church. This was a spiritual matter, not a secular one, although many people might be unaware of the distinction.

Over the years, I came to see that being a Catholic requires obedience to traditions and a degree of humility, two virtues that are not touted in the secular world today. For someone like me, who had been taught in graduate school to come up with rebuttals to nearly every idea and to criticize nearly everything, humility and obedience were major challenges.

It was, however, rather delightful to be married, again, to my dear husband and to have Father Pat and some friends over for lasagna and chocolate cake afterward. A few months later, Jef was received into the Catholic Church at the Easter Vigil Mass, with two of the Missionary of Charity sisters beaming in the congregation. After anointing him with blessed oil in the sacrament of confirmation, Father Pat called Jef by the new name of Francesco, which my husband had chosen in honor of the well-known friar from Assisi.

Now we could approach the altar together each Sunday, and when the priest raised the Host before us and said, "The Body of Christ", we could say "Amen" in agreement. As the years passed, I realized that no matter what was going on in my life, receiving the Eucharist always brought a sense of comfort. There were times when the music in church was impossible and the sermons dull, but the heart of Sunday was the Eucharist, and I would put up with anything to encounter Christ there.

It would be many years before I would find a passage in the letters of Flannery O'Connor that best expressed how I felt. She wrote to a friend about a dinner party where people were expressing opinions on the Eucharist:

> Mrs. Broadwater said when she was a child and received the Host, she thought of it as the Holy Ghost, He being the "most portable" person of the Trinity; now she thought of it as a symbol and implied that it was a pretty good one. I then said, in a very shaky voice, "Well, if it's a symbol, to hell with it." [3]

Flannery went on to say, "That was all the defense I was capable of but I realize now that this is all I will ever be able to say about it, outside of a story, except that it is the center of existence for me; all the rest of life is expendable."

The Eucharist was also the center for me. And I kept wondering why belief in the Real Presence was not omnipresent among Christians. After all, if people were willing to embrace the miracle of God humbling himself to become a human being, and a tiny baby at that, then why couldn't they see echoes of that same miracle in bread and wine mysteriously becoming Christ's Body and Blood? A symbol did not die on the Cross but a real Person, and that Person had left a real sacrament, not a symbol, to show his love.

12

Nibbling on the Sacramental Cake

"We met Mother Teresa!" reads my journal entry for June 17, 1995. The sisters had invited about a hundred people to the official opening of the Gift of Grace Home, where Mother would be present. On the big day, we climbed out of bed at 5 A.M. and headed over to Saint Charles Avenue, where we discovered a huge media blitz under way, with crowds gathering and cameras rolling.

After our names were checked off the list of volunteers, we squeezed into the crowded dining room and waited with the others. Before long, a line of sisters processed into the room, all wearing identical white saris with blue stripes. At that very moment, one of the demons from my past reared its head, as I found myself wondering, rather cynically, if all the hoopla about Mother Teresa wasn't just a fabrication of the media.

Yes, her sisters were some of the sweetest, holiest women I had ever met, but was it really possible that a woman as well-known as Mother Teresa could have remained immune from the egoism that typically infected celebrities? Besides, I thought, rather grumpily, nothing could ever match the experience of seeing the manatees in Cedar Key.

Soon Mother Teresa was passing right by us. As she did, a woman reached out to touch the hem of Mother's sari, and I remember thinking how annoyed I would have been at that gesture. But Mother Teresa turned and smiled at the woman and gently took her hands. Then, in a split second, Mother Teresa turned and her eyes met mine. She was very stooped over, and her face was covered in wrinkles, but her eyes radiated an unusual clear, childlike, innocent quality.

In that moment, completely out of the blue, I saw an image superimposed on this holy woman's face: the curious, innocent eyes of the manatee! The moment passed quickly, but I wondered later if God might be playing a joke on me. It was as if he were saying, "You didn't think anything could beat the manatee experience, huh? Well, what about this?" Years later, I was comforted to discover that a brilliant and very holy man, Joseph Cardinal Ratzinger (now Pope Benedict XVI), agreed with me about God's sense of humor when he wrote: "Sometimes [God] gives you something like a nudge and says, Don't take yourself so seriously!" [1]

After Mass, the crowds lined up to get a blessing from Mother Teresa. She placed her hands gently on each person's head and whispered, "God bless you." When it was my turn, I was so nervous that, after she blessed me, I gave her a little pat and said, "God bless you too." One of the little sisters, standing nearby, broke into a big smile, which I knew meant: "Oh look, there's Lorraine, giving a blessing to Mother!"

For the next few months, life was very good. We continued helping the sisters with little repairs and would sometimes drive the residents of the Gift of Grace house to the shopping center. We sang in the choir at Saint Thomas More and looked forward to Sunday Mass as the cornerstone of the week. Our lives finally had a definite spiritual center. And then, out of nowhere, everything came crashing down.

Jef developed a painful and debilitating back ailment that his doctors could not accurately diagnose or treat. He could no longer help the sisters with repair jobs or do his usual chores at home. Even going to Mass became impossible for him because sitting in the pews was so painful. There seemed to be no medical hope on the horizon. Doctors hinted at a disk problem but offered no solutions.

One Sunday, I couldn't keep the tears at bay as I sat in the pew at church. All I could think about was my husband at home, depressed and in pain. In a very childish way, I had believed that his conversion, and my return to the fold, would somehow protect us from sorrowful times like these. My peculiar mentality was best summed up by "Didn't I pay my dues?" My parents had died, and that had been a terrible time for me. Also, we had given so much to God in the past year. Why wasn't he keeping up his end of the bargain?

I was still largely unschooled in the finer points of Catholic theology and didn't understand why apparently good people had to suffer. But as I prayed for my husband and took care of him, I was slowly realizing that suffering can be the catalyst that changes hearts. As Pope Benedict XVI said, through suffering, "we can acquire freedom and maturity and above all else a capacity for sympathy with others." [2] My husband had taken care of me for many years: cooking us special meals, repairing the house, working in the yard, and, most of all, cheering me up when I had the blues. Now the tables had turned. It was an extremely difficult time, but my own heart was forced to grow a bit larger.

After Mass that day, I told Father John Murphy, the associate pastor, that I was at my wits' end about my husband, who couldn't even come to church because he was in so much pain. Father John immediately promised to stop by later that day to check on him. More important, Father brought Communion and holy oils with him, and Jef received the anointing of the sick, also known as extreme unction. They talked for about an hour, and Jef later seemed less despondent.

First it had been Father Pat Mulhern welcoming me back to the Church, then Father Joseph extending God's mercy in the confessional, then Father John Fallon's words in the chapel, and now Father John Murphy's visit: I was beginning to sense how a priest really does stand in for Christ in people's lives and can bring God's love and grace into the darkest corners.

Jef's back problem was the proverbial wake-up call in our lives. We had two mortgages and other debts and began to worry that he might be unable to work. We also realized that it was extremely unlikely that we would ever move to our beloved island, Cedar Key. There were no jobs for us there, and we also were troubled by the island's lack of a Catholic church. We were involved in the congregation at Saint Thomas More, where we sang in the choir and helped out with various ministries. We were reluctant to move to a town where the nearest Catholic church was thirty miles away.

We were also starting to examine the ways we spent money. Donna, a Christian friend at my office, had introduced us to the book *Your Money or Your Life*, which stressed living frugally and sanely and learning to get out of debt. We were aware of how simply the sisters lived at the Gift of Grace Home, and we knew they modeled themselves after Christ. Now we began to wonder if we were being called to follow Christ more closely. He had warned about the spiritual danger of having two masters in life. Was our attachment to the vacation home becoming another master for us?

In August 1997, after much soul-searching, we sold our beloved Marsh Nest and also gave away our boat. As we closed the door on our old dream, it was a sad moment but also one mixed with relief. We felt that we were shedding excess baggage in our lives and also forestalling the potential appearance of the proverbial wolf at our door.

My feelings about Catholicism were still guarded. I loved the Mass and the sacraments, but I still clung tightly to my opinions about social and political issues. Despite my own painful experience, I still thought women should have the right to abortion and could not accept the Church's apparently old-fashioned stance on this and other issues.

I was woefully ignorant of the reasoning behind the Church's positions and did not realize that the information was readily available in the catechism and elsewhere. Instead of researching the background and history of Catholic teachings, I clung stubbornly to my own opinions and thought of myself as somehow more knowledgeable than the saints and Fathers of the Church. I was, after all, a modern-day woman!

I still was hesitant about telling non-Catholic friends that I had returned to the Catholic fold; I kept imagining an older version of myself peeking over my shoulder and laughing at me. Whenever the topic of religion came up, I was quick to assure people that, although I was Catholic, I was still a feminist and didn't accept many of the old-fashioned teachings of the Church. In short, I took pride in being a "cafeteria Catholic" par excellence, blithely choosing some teachings and rejecting others. I didn't realize it, but my full conversion into the faith would occur many years in the future.

In my journal, I wrote that I saw the Church as consisting of layers, with the Mass and sacraments at the core, and the admonitions about such things as abortion, euthanasia, and contraception as icing on the sacramental cake. "Do I dislike the icing?" I wrote. "Parts of it, yes. But would I therefore throw away the cake? Never." I went on to say, in my particularly arrogant fashion, that I loved the Church, "despite her flaws". It would be years before I would understand that my analogy itself was flawed: Teachings on faith and morals are inherent to Catholicism, rather than window dressing that can be removed.

In truth, I often felt lonely as a woman who had returned to Catholicism. Many of my nonchurchgoing friends shied away from talking about God in everyday conversations. "It's much more acceptable to be cynical and sarcastic and to poke fun at people who believe," I wrote, and then added that I understood this tendency, "since I had been one of the worst ones for doing just that."

Fortunately, Jef and I were making new friends at church, people who saw the Mass as the centerpiece of their Sundays, and the Eucharist as the heart of their lives. One couple, Pam and Chris, had a little boy named Stephen, then two years old. When their little girl, Sarah, was born in 1998, they paid us the ultimate compliment by asking if we would become her godparents. Our involvement as "Aunt Lorraine" and "Uncle Jef" in their children's lives has continued to be a joy to this day.

❧

For years I had promised myself that "someday" I would write a book, but by the time I got home from my publications job, after a sixty-mile round-trip drive, I was exhausted. As we continued to monitor our spending, we began running classes at church to help others live more simply. I started questioning my high-stress lifestyle. I wondered if the frantic energy I was pouring into my job might be making my old dream of writing a book impossible.

We continued the somewhat painful task of paring back our expenses and living frugally. As the months passed and our savings grew, a new dream took shape in my heart: I would quit my job and become a free-lance writer. *Southline* newspaper had gone out of business by this time, but I was eager to try my hand with other venues.

One Sunday, after Communion, I heard a voice in my head that I knew was not my own: "Whatever you want spiritually, I will give you." At that point, there were no material objects that I yearned for; I just wanted the great spiritual gift of having more free time to devote to writing.

My publications job had turned sour after my beloved boss had retired, and there were mornings when I would cry on the long commute to work. As I envisioned a different life, I began writing short reflections and trying to get them published. On a whim, I sent an article to a journal called *Sacred Journey* and was delighted when it was accepted. I also sent an editorial to the *Atlanta-Journal Constitution* about ways that people without children could enjoy a child-centered holiday like Christmas. Much to my amazement, this article also was accepted.

After a few more hits, I decided that God was giving me the go-ahead to leave my job. After quitting in February 1999, I began writing columns on a regular basis for the Faith and Values section of the *Atlanta Journal-Constitution*, which was edited at that time by Ron Feinberg. I also wrote for the Jesuit magazine *America* and would eventually become a regular columnist with the *Georgia Bulletin*, the news-paper of the Catholic Archdiocese of Atlanta.

I loved being a free-lancer. Waking up and making a cup of coffee and heading to the computer in my pajamas and fuzzy pig slippers—now that was bliss! No more long com-mutes, no more meetings, no more overflowing in-boxes and office misery. The prison door had opened, and I was flying free! Of course, I had no way to know that a major catastrophe was headed in my direction, and in a few months it would send me falling to my knees.

13

"Throw Yourself into Christ's Arms"

After many prayers, Jef's back ailment ended as mysteriously as it had begun, and he was soon his old feisty self again. He happily resumed his old duties: tending the garden, making wine, shopping at the farmer's market, and cooking us gourmet meals. When I started writing at home, he began drawing and painting again, as he had in childhood days.

Our Saturdays soon took on a comfortable rhythm that has continued to this day: He headed down to his basement studio and painted, while I sat nearby at the computer, writing. Before long, our house filled up with his lovely oil paintings and cut-out wooden creatures, ranging from fish and birds to angels and dragons.

And then, just when things seemed to be going in the absolutely right direction, a major catastrophe was unleashed. On May 18, 2000, I was diagnosed with breast cancer, and the bottom fell out of our happy little world. On the day the doctor telephoned me with the devastating news, Jef was on a business trip out of town and I was all alone. The first person I called was my best friend, Pam, who raced over with her daughter, Sarah, then two. As Pam hugged me, my little goddaughter watched from the couch and then toddled over to grab my knees. Even in the midst of horror, a faint glimmer of light was appearing.

When my column about the diagnosis appeared in the *Atlanta Journal-Constitution*, hundreds of readers e-mailed to encourage me and assure me of their prayers. My friends at church and my family also rallied, and soon I was inundated with e-mails, cards, letters, calls, flowers, chocolates, and other outpourings of love.

Father Pat had retired from Saint Thomas More in 1999, and a new priest, Father Frank X. Richardson, had become pastor. I can remember walking around in a daze one day before Mass and how he came up to me and very gently said, "You will be fine." I was not ready to fully believe him at that moment, but I never forgot the tone of certainty in his voice and how that comforted me.

The surgeon that I went to see had a Bible in the waiting room, which I took to be a good sign, and I mustered up the courage to ask if he would say a prayer with me before surgery. On May 30, moments before I succumbed to the anesthesia, Dr. John S. Kennedy fulfilled his promise, and we prayed the Lord's Prayer together. I was terrified of surgery and was afraid that I would die, which probably explains why my first question in the recovery room was, "Is this heaven?" I am sure the nurses all had a good laugh over that question.

After the surgery, Dr. Kennedy had good news to report: The tumor had been discovered very early and had been small. I would be spared chemotherapy, but I would have to undergo seven weeks of daily radiation therapy and would be on medication for the next five years. The weeks that followed are a mere blur in my memory. Somehow I got up, dressed, ate breakfast, and made it through each day, although at some point, I simply had to sit on the couch and weep. In spite of Dr. Kennedy's assurance that my prognosis was excellent, I still felt that I was reliving the nightmare preceding my mother's death and was frightened that my fate would mirror hers.

In the midst of this storm, a minor miracle occurred: I received a letter from an editor at Resurrection Press who had seen my articles in *America*. She wondered if I might like to put together a collection of my columns to become a book. When I opened the letter, I was so weary and still so much in the throes of "poor me" that I didn't grasp the full import of her words. Later, I realized what this letter meant: My dream of writing a book was finally going to come true.

The book became the center of my life for the next few months, and the irony of the name "Resurrection Press" was not lost on me, because the book somewhat revived me from my sorrows. Published in March 2002, the book was dedicated to my husband and named *Grace Notes* after my mother.

My faith was still rather childish, and at times, I was angry at God for the huge disruption that cancer caused in my life. Once again, I found myself wondering, "Didn't I pay my dues?" At other times, I asked God, "Why me?" After all, I had been so careful about my weight, exercise, and vitamin-taking for so long. In some ways, I felt that God had let me down because he had not protected me. I was extremely egocentric and rarely thought about people suffering from much worse ailments, and with far fewer complaints.

Fortunately, though, my commitment to Christ was deeply rooted, and this latest battle would not tear me away from him. I had seen life from the perspective of a nonbeliever and through the eyes of a Christian, and I knew that I would never give up my relationship with Christ again, even if that meant enduring, at times, what Saint John of the Cross had called "the dark night of the soul".

I was stricken with a sense of urgency about my life. Would the cancer come back? How much time did I really have left? No one can answer this question, of course, but cancer brings it to the forefront of one's heart. For years, I had thought about getting a spiritual director but had procrastinated. Now I knew it was time to take action, so I asked the advice of a friend, Father Balappa Selvaraj, who highly recommended a local priest.

The letter that I wrote to Father Richard Lopez was similar to one that I might have sent my heavenly Father: I wrote that he would surely be too busy to see me, but I thought I'd ask him anyway. Father Lopez wrote back to say that he would be honored to see me and added that he wanted me to know something about him. His favorite saint was Thérèse of Lisieux, who is known as the Little Flower and whose path to God is called "the Little Way".

I discovered that Saint Thérèse's spirituality had inspired Mother Teresa, who also believed that what is important in life is not making a huge splash but doing small things with great love. In *The Story of a Soul*, Thérèse describes the humble path of spiritual childhood, based on Christ's admonition that entering heaven meant having a conversion of heart and becoming like a child. Children can do simple, humble things to show their love for others, and that was the path that Thérèse took.

Saint Thérèse's approach to suffering seemed light-years more advanced than my own attitude. She died in 1897, at the age of twenty-four, after a long and painful struggle with tuberculosis. Still, she had believed, in a childlike and trusting way, that everything that happens to us comes from the hand of our heavenly Father. Although I was not fully ready to accept her point of view, it impressed me nonetheless and showed me a very different approach to hardship. On the back of a holy card depicting Saint Thérèse that Father Lopez sent me were these words:

> Everything is a grace, everything is the direct effect of our Father's love, difficulties, contradictions, humiliations, all the soul's miseries, her burdens, her needs, everything, because through them, she learns humility, realizes her weakness. Everything is a grace because everything is God's gift. Whatever be the character of life or its unexpected events—to the heart that loves, all is well. [1]

It was a cloudy Halloween day in 2000 when I drove to Saint Pius X Catholic High School, where Father Richard Lopez taught religion. In his classroom, where he had been preparing for the next day's class, he greeted me with an enthusiastic handshake and a humorous apology about the disorganized state of his desk. In some ways his Latin good looks reminded me of the men in my family, and as we talked a bit about our lives, I discovered we had much in common. Like me, he had family in New York and had grown up in Florida. He had also majored in philosophy in college.

At first, we talked mostly about the cancer diagnosis. I was depressed and would often burst into tears as I unburdened myself to him. I confessed that I didn't feel, on a heartfelt basis, that God loved me, nor had I ever felt loved by my earthly father. During our weekly sessions, Father Lopez always gave me his full attention and assured me of God's love.

"You have to throw yourself into Christ's arms, over and over again", he said that first day, and this image sustained me for a long time. This man's devotion to Jesus Christ was strikingly real and apparent, and he conveyed Christ's love through his own attention to me. Father Lopez had no doubt seen people like me hundreds of times before: devastated over their particular burdens, despite the fact that millions of others were struggling with much worse situations.

Like them, I was coming face-to-face with that big question, the same one that I had relied on when I attempted to disprove God's existence back in my days as a philosophy teacher: Why does a good and merciful God allow suffering? It would take us months to explore this one, but I was eager to begin.

It took me a long time to rid myself of the image of an angry God, the old man in the sky who was seeking vengeance on people for their sins. Father Lopez assured me, time and again, that God is merciful: "He is always gazing at you with love." In a book that he recommended, I encountered for the first time the notion that God might actually weep over the paths that his children were choosing: Gerald Vann wrote, "Wherever there is suffering in the world, there is the sorrow of God." [2]

With Father Lopez's help, I began to glimpse the mysterious connection between human freedom and suffering. I discovered that, according to traditional Catholic theology, God did not create human beings as robots that would always make the right choices but instead as creatures with free will. Thus, much of the world's suffering results from crime and war, a result of terrible choices that human beings freely make. Other suffering comes from the flawed fabric of our fallen natural world, into which earthquakes, tsunamis, and diseases are interwoven.

I realized that even a question like "Why did God cause me to get cancer?" was ridiculous. Yes, it is true that God had allowed the illness to occur, because he is in charge of the world, and nothing happens that he does not know about. But to say that God causes a particular person's cancer is absurd. Perhaps a better description of causes might be my own past choices, made in ignorance, such as my decision to use birth control pills and then hormone-replacement therapy at various times in my life.

When I confessed my shame over my wild and sinful past, Father Lopez asked a simple question: "What is greater in your life—your past or the power of God to work through your past?" He assured me, time and again, that God's grace can transform any situation. He also told me that depression can be a cross for many people and advised me, whenever I was having a melancholy day, to offer my suffering to God.

At first I just didn't get it. What did "offer it up" really mean? I had heard that expression when I was a child but never could make sense of it. Gradually, through my sessions with Father Lopez, I began to see that Christianity, among all religions, has a unique answer for what traditionally is called the "problem of evil" and that "offering it up" plays a role in it.

Christ's death on the Cross shows that God can take any suffering and any evil and turn it around. That was the ultimate meaning of the Crucifixion: An innocent man had experienced an agonizing and terrible death, which had given way to new life in the Resurrection. Christ himself had offered up his suffering on the Cross. He had given his life out of love for mankind.

According to traditional Catholic theology, those who love Christ will not be spared from suffering, but he will help them bear it. In the end, Christianity offers the only satisfying solution to the problem that I grappled with when I was teaching philosophy: Why do good people suffer? During the Crucifixion, God himself experienced the absolute depths of human suffering. But the final chapter of that story was not the tomb but the transformation that occurred through the Resurrection. As Alice von Hildebrand so eloquently stated it, "From a supernatural point of view, there is nothing, absolutely nothing, which cannot be turned to God's glory. *Every defeat can become a victory.*" [3]

I began to see that God could transform my mental anguish. This was a mystical situation, obviously. God wasn't an accountant, keeping tabs on suffering and figuring out the pluses and minuses in everyone's life. But if I could prayerfully offer God my emotional struggles with cancer, my agonizing would not be in vain. Somehow, somewhere, someone else could benefit from my suffering.

One day, when I was at the hospital, feeling sorry for myself, I saw an old man in a wheelchair. He was hooked up to oxygen and looked as though he was in very bad shape. Nearby was his faithful daughter, pushing the wheelchair and looking quite downtrodden herself. In that moment, I whispered a silent prayer: "Lord, I offer you my suffering this day for the betterment of that old man and his daughter." Finally, I was beginning to understand what it meant to "offer it up".

❧

"Continually turning inward toward God" was Flannery O'Connor's description of the conversion process. She did not think of conversion as being "once and for all, and that's that", [4] and I have to agree wholeheartedly. For me, returning to Catholicism has been a work in progress for many years, and it is still continuing today, with the help of my spiritual advisor. As Father Lopez has suggested books and articles for me to read, I've discovered the reasoning behind the Church's teachings on many moral topics that so often are misunderstood in the secular press. Together we have explored the Catholic stance on abortion, euthanasia, in vitro fertilization, embryonic stem cell research, and other issues.

Once I understood the theological and historical under-pinnings of Church declarations and recognized that teach-ings about life form a seamless web, I realized that I could not, in good faith, remain a "cafeteria Catholic". I saw that it didn't matter whether I thought of myself as a "modern-day woman". As Flannery O'Connor had commented, "If you're a Catholic you believe what the Church teaches and the [social] climate makes no difference." [5]

As she put it, Christ himself speaks through the Church. This does not mean that the pope can't make mistakes in his day-to-day life and commit sins, since he is, after all, human. But when he makes declarations, *ex cathedra*, on matters of faith and morals, he does so with Christ's guidance, and these teachings are marked with the stamp of truth. I finally real-ized that protecting and cherishing life from the moment of conception until natural death is an inherent part of Cath-olic teachings. Believing that the divine image is present in even so tiny a speck as an embryo is as vital as embracing the Real Presence of Christ in the Eucharist.

Through my discussions with Father Lopez, I also dis-covered a brand of feminism that was very different from the model I had once followed: The group called Feminists for Life is both pro-woman *and* pro-child and deplores abor-tion as an act of violence against women as well as against children. Despite my own examination of feminism in grad-uate school days, I had somehow managed to miss a vital piece of history, namely, that the suffragettes themselves had not advocated legalizing abortion. Instead, they had seen abortion as a tragic example of the way society failed to help women in need.

Through Father Lopez, I met an Emory University professor, Elizabeth Fox-Genovese, who was active in Feminists for Life. Betsey had started out as a radical feminist, defending abortion, until she had a conversion experience of her own. She went on to create quite a stir among pro-abortion feminists with her book, *Feminism Is Not the Story of My Life*, in which she criticized feminism for failing to take into account the ordinary lives of everyday women for whom motherhood was not seen as a burden but as a gift. Betsey also had been mentored by Father Lopez in her search for truth with a capital *T* and had been received into the Catholic Church while still heading the women's studies institute at Emory University.

Gradually, I came to see that Catholicism recognizes an inherent dignity in women, especially in light of the great respect paid to the Virgin Mary. It is true that the Church teaches that God created men and women with different natures, but this teaching does not sanction women's subjugation by men. In a book review, Betsey suggested that radical feminists balked at the possibility that one could be both pro-woman and Catholic. She believed this was due to an inherent disconnect in feminism concerning the notion of service, which is the core of Christianity for both men and women. Further, she said that many proponents of women's rights fail to realize that rights include responsibilities and duties, especially to children. The unrestricted freedom that feminists want for women, she wrote, "disconcertingly resembles equal membership in what [Pope John Paul II] called 'the culture of death'".[6]

Longing for Flannery

About two years after the cancer diagnosis, I rather reluctantly began a new writing venture. Although I had little
desire to dwell on what had happened, I had a strong sense
that I should write a book about my spiritual journey with
cancer in a way that might encourage other women in the
same situation. Despite my initial reticence, I eventually found
solace in this project, because as I pored over Scripture to
find encouraging messages that might help others, my own
emotional healing began.

When I sent the manuscript to Ave Maria Press, a kind
and helpful editor, Dan Driscoll, had faith that it would
make a fine book, and he called me one morning to say
that it had been accepted. *Why Me? Why Now? Finding Hope
When You Have Breast Cancer* made its debut in 2003, and
when I held the book in my hands for the first time, I
realized that God had shown me how to take even something as bitter as cancer and use it for a good purpose.

There are still times, of course, when I feel that I have
finally "paid my dues" and can now sit back and expect life
to go smoothly. However, I have seen enough of other
people's lives to know that suffering is something that comes

and goes, and no one is spared. More and more, I am seeing the truth of Flannery O'Connor's words: "[People] think faith is a big electric blanket, when of course it is the cross." [1]

When I came back to the Church, I was looking for the blanket and was quite surprised when I discovered the cross. Today, I've had a long respite from the emotional suffering of a cancer diagnosis, but I know it is not realistic to expect to avoid the cross in the future. Of course, I am hoping that, when I am next called upon to carry it, I will rely on the lessons I've learned so far and keep my eyes fixed on Christ.

There are so many people who reveal what it means to bear suffering graciously and in a Christlike fashion. One lady I know has been stricken with multiple sclerosis and heroically endures the debilitating symptoms with little complaint. Another woman cares around the clock for a spouse who is almost completely helpless from Parkinson's disease. I envision these people bent beneath the Cross and believe their strength comes from a supernatural, not an earthly, source. Someone helped Christ carry his Cross, and surely he helps his children with theirs.

I have also discovered companions in the saints, especially Edith Stein. Born into a Jewish family, Stein became an atheist in her teens and received her doctorate in philosophy in 1916. Six years later, because of her thirst for absolute truth, she converted to Catholicism, and she eventually entered a Carmelite monastery, where she took the name Sister Teresa Benedicta of the Cross. In 1939, in her self-offering to Christ, Stein wrote: "Already now I joyfully accept the death which God has destined for me in complete submission to his most holy Will." [2] Stein modeled the essence of Christ's selfless service when she was transported to a concentration camp, where she devoted herself to taking care of others. She eventually died in the gas chambers at Auschwitz.

Then there are the people unwittingly adding to Christ's suffering by denying him, and, oh, how they remind me of myself in my younger years! At a recent luncheon, for example, some people asserted that they were Christians, and had been raised as such, but they ardently insisted that Christ was not God. Instead, one said, and all nodded in agreement, "He was a good man." A bitter comment by Flannery O'Connor came to mind: She said that if Christ was merely a man, the Crucifixion was an act of justice.[3] Her point, which echoes C. S. Lewis in *Mere Christianity*, is that if Christ were not God, as he claimed to be, then he was a liar, and there would be no reason to respect him as a "good man".

I often think of Flannery in such situations and can imagine her praying for the people at the luncheon. So often, I have wished that she were still alive, so that I might write her a letter and ask her advice. "You probably have not imagined what it is to write as a Catholic," she wrote in a letter, way back in 1954, "knowing that most of the people who read you will think what you believe is utter rubbish."[4] Flannery described herself rather succinctly as a fiction writer "who believes that there was a fall, has been a Redemption, and will be a judgment"—in short, she described herself as a Catholic.[5]

For the past few years, I have been writing a column called "Grace Notes" for the Faith and Values section of the *Atlanta Journal-Constitution*, and I have discovered that representing Catholicism in the secular press is a sweet rose that comes with plenty of thorns. Many readers are remarkably encouraging in their e-mails, letters, and phone calls, but there are times when one of my columns sparks bitter controversy—and the proverbial fur starts to fly. It is then that I especially long for a conversation with Flannery.

Some readers disagree respectfully and state their points in a calm fashion, and we will have a congenial give-and-take of ideas via e-mail. But there are also angry readers, who are quick to pounce on anything that smacks of God and religion. Some of the atheists remind me so much of my former self. They will dash off furious letters to the editor—and to me—whenever they suspect I am trying to prove the existence of God. Then there are the Christians who are dead-set against anything that resembles Catholic dogma and will rush to their computers to try to set me straight.

Some Protestants complain that I can't possibly speak as a true Christian, since they dismiss Catholicism as somehow "unbiblical". One reader raged that I was a "virulent Catholic", and another tried to put me in my place by labeling me "Sister Mary Lorraine", who based her ideas on the *Baltimore Catechism*, as if that were a terrible crime indeed. After a column about my conversion, in which I mentioned Thomas Merton, G. K. Chesterton, and Flannery O'Connor, one reader took me to task for quoting "dead Catholics" instead of the Bible.

Some people are eager to pigeonhole anyone who writes a column as either conservative or liberal, without realizing that a faithful Catholic can be both. For example, the Church's reverence for life puts her in the conservative camp, while her concern for the poor and her opposition to unjust wars aligns her more with the liberal camp. When I write about the war in Iraq, some readers will dash off notes labeling me a liberal, and when I write about abortion, others brand me as a conservative.

On the days when the irate e-mails are flowing in, I sometimes consider giving up entirely on writing. But then a note will show up from a reader who had turned her back on God, and she will say that a column helped her reconsider. Another note came from a woman who had been fantasizing about having an affair, but a column that emphasized keeping our promises made her think again. When I feel downtrodden, Father Lopez always encourages me and reminds me that writing is my vocation. I also take to heart Flannery's advice to a friend who was a fledgling writer: "Any criticism at all which depresses you to the extent that you feel you cannot ever write anything worth anything is from the devil and to subject yourself to it is for you an occasion of sin." [6]

Writing for newspapers is a great privilege and a tremendous responsibility, and I often pray that God will help me express myself in a way that will bring people closer to him. My prayer is this: "Please help me to do your will in my writing." Over the years, I've had to conclude that God's plan for me includes more than writing, since I have been invited, numerous times, to speak at various churches in Atlanta. At first, I refused, because I was nervous about public speaking, but once I realized that giving talks might be another way to serve God, I have accepted more invitations, and my stage fright has diminished.

I am always humbled by how gracious people are when I do give talks, and I often get a kick out of some of their reactions. For example, one lady commented that she expected me to be a lot taller, given my photo, even though the newspaper runs only my headshot. Another lady said she expected me to be blonde. Some affirm that I look much better than my photo, and as for the ones who think otherwise, they are evidently kind enough to keep their thoughts to themselves.

Writing takes many hours a day, and so does background reading. Jef and I work mornings in the Pitts Theology Library at Emory University at modestly paying jobs, which give us freedom to do creative work in the afternoons. When I'm not at the computer, I may be hunkered down in my blue Queen Anne chair, perusing a theology book with our elderly cat, Tinker Bell, purring on my lap. On Saturday evenings, after I've spent all day writing, my husband sits in his matching chair and listens as I read my work aloud. He will alert me if something sounds rough around the edges, and when I get upset over readers' reactions, he helps me put things in perspective.

In 2003, we left Saint Thomas More Church because we longed for a more traditional liturgy. This we found at Sacred Heart Church and Saint John Chrysostom Melkite Catholic Church. The latter is home to many people of Middle Eastern descent, and many of the dark-eyed children there remind me of my cousins when they were young. The fact that Jef and I never had children remains a source of regret for me, especially now that we are at an age when some friends are having grandchildren. On holidays like Christmas and Easter, I picture us standing on the sidelines of the big dance of life, in which children play such a key role. Still, I am very grateful that my sister now has six grandchildren, and when my husband and I visit them, and vice versa, we are immersed in a very loving and sustaining "communion of saints".

Edith Stein mentioned her belief in the possibility of "spiritual motherhood" in her writings, and perhaps that is the kind that I am enjoying, since the money that comes in from free-lance writing has enabled me to support children overseas through Catholic Near East Welfare Association. My hope is that God will continue to bless our work, so that in the future we might post more smiling faces on the refrigerator door.

I feel that I am doing the work that God called me to do, long ago, when I was growing up in Miami and yearning to "someday" be a writer. It seems that writing is the thing that I was evidently put on earth to do, and, in truth, it is the only thing that I do reasonably well. So I will, with God's help, continue doing it, as long as it is humanly possible.

Epilogue

"Everything Is a Grace"

Thomas Merton and Flannery O'Connor have been my ex officio spiritual directors on my journey. It is true that they both died in the 1960s, when I was busy carousing at the University of Florida, but they are part of the communion of saints, and they can continue doing good deeds on earth. "I am perfectly sure I shall not stay inactive in heaven",[1] wrote Saint Thérèse of Lisieux, and I think that comment applies to Merton and O'Connor as well.

I believe these two writers are continuing to affect the lives of people on earth, not just by their prayers in heaven, but by the works they have left behind. In *The Living Bread*, Merton writes that Jesus knew each of us alive today—our sins, our weaknesses, and our inmost hearts—as he was suffering on the Cross.[2] As God, he knows everything, and he exists in eternal, not human, time. Merton's distinction between eternal and human time helped me solve a mystery from my childhood: Frankly, I was quite perplexed when the nuns told the children that Jesus had died for our sins.

I had wondered: How could that be possible? After all, I wasn't alive when Jesus died on the Cross, so I hadn't started sinning yet! It took an adult understanding to grasp Merton's distinction and to read the words of Gerald Vann in

The Pain of Christ and the Sorrow of God: "Christ did not die for the sins that were then being committed or had been committed in the past, it was the total evil of the world, past, present and future, that was responsible for Calvary." [3] When I sin today, then, "I as surely crucify God as did the soldiers on the hill of Golgotha." [4]

Of course, I understood that the things we do in the present affect the future, but this mystical sense of time, in which the present can touch the past, was certainly not something I could grasp as a child. And now that I am aware of mystical time, there is no escaping a painful conclusion: During the many years when I was waging my bitter vendetta against the Church, I was contributing greatly to the accumulation of the world's sins and thus intensifying Christ's suffering.

Still, Father Lopez has helped me learn the most important lesson about Christianity, the one which makes it unique from all other religions. It is a religion based on grace. As the story of the woman washing Jesus' feet with her tears so poignantly shows, God's love and forgiveness are freely given, even to the worst sinners.

I also believe that we can make amends for our earlier misdeeds. Confession, of course, offers the way to obtain complete forgiveness of the sins for which we are truly sorry. But, afterwards, in addition, we can offset some of the terrible things we have done in our lives through daily sacrifices, large and small, and by being charitable to others.

In response to a college student struggling with the question of God's existence, Flannery mentioned the advice that Gerard Manley Hopkins had offered an agnostic friend: "Give alms." [5] She advised the student to put aside his intellectual convolutions, because God is discovered through loving others. As she put it, we experience God as we learn to love the divine image in human beings.

Love, however, is not an insurance policy against suffering, and even the most sincere and dedicated Christians, such as Flannery O'Connor, may experience terrible hardships. She developed lupus, an incurable and painful disease, and died at age thirty-nine, after a long decline. Despite her illness, Flannery managed to continue writing letters to friends who needed spiritual advice, and to write her stories. She was a beautiful example of a person whose life modeled the words of Saint Paul: "Power is made perfect in weakness" (2 Cor 12:9).

All these years later, I am still trying to put into practice that simple formula that I memorized as a child: God made us to know, love, and serve him in this world and to be happy with him in the next. In his first letter, Saint John wrote, "He who does not love does not know God; for God is love" (1 Jn 4:8). Since God is love, it seems to follow that life on earth is a gigantic love affair and an adventure played out between God and his children.

And whatever future adventures come my way, I pray that God will help me to love him more deeply and more fully realize the depth of his love for me. I also pray that I will put more trust in the words of Saint Thérèse: "Everything is a grace." [6]

NOTES

INTRODUCTION

1. C. S. Lewis, *Surprised by Joy* (San Diego: Harcourt Brace and Company, 1955), 191.

CHAPTER FOUR
LIFE IN SIN CITY

1. Flannery O'Connor, Letter to Alfred Corn, May 30, 1962, in *Collected Works* (New York: The Library of America, 1988), 1165.
2. Ibid.
3. Ibid.

CHAPTER FIVE
VENDETTA AGAINST GOD

1. Flannery O'Connor, Letter to A., August 28, 1955, in *Collected Works* (New York: The Library of America, 1988), 949.
2. Leo Tolstoy, *Leo Tolstoy: Spiritual Writings*, ed. Charles E. Moore (Maryknoll, N.Y.: Orbis Books, 2006), 54.

CHAPTER SEVEN
THE MIST OF TEARS

1. Francis Thompson, "The Hound of Heaven", in *Selected Poems of Francis Thompson* (London: Methuen and Company, 1909), 51, lines 1–5.

CHAPTER NINE
TWITCHES UPON THE THREAD

1. G. K. Chesterton, *The Innocence of Father Brown* (London: Cassell and Company, 1911), 89.
2. C. S. Lewis, *Surprised by Joy* (San Diego: Harcourt Brace and Company, 1955), 191.

3. Thomas Merton, *The Seven Storey Mountain* (New York: Harcourt Brace Jovanovich, 1976), 13.

4. Ibid.

5. Lewis, *Surprised by Joy*, 190.

6. Thomas à Kempis, *The Imitation of Christ*, bk. 2, chap. 4 (New York: Catholic Book Publishing Company, 1993), 74.

CHAPTER TEN
CHINKS IN MY FEMINIST ARMOR

1. Flannery O'Connor, Letter to A., August 9, 1955, in *Collected Works* (New York: The Library of America, 1988), 945.

2. C. S. Lewis, *Surprised by Joy* (San Diego: Harcourt Brace and Company, 1955), 236.

3. Thomas Merton, *The Seven Storey Mountain* (New York: Harcourt Brace Jovanovich, 1976), 121.

4. Lewis, *Surprised by Joy*, 228.

5. Ibid., 229.

CHAPTER ELEVEN
FAREWELL TO THE LITTLE SOUL

1. Alice von Hildebrand, *The Privilege of Being a Woman* (Ypsilanti, Michigan: Veritas Press of Ave Maria University, 2002), 33.

2. Ibid., 96.

3. Flannery O'Connor, Letter to A., December 16, 1955, in *Collected Works* (New York: The Library of America, 1988), 977.

CHAPTER TWELVE
NIBBLING ON THE SACRAMENTAL CAKE

1. Joseph Cardinal Ratzinger, *God and the World*, trans. Henry Taylor (San Francisco: Ignatius Press, 2002), 19.

2. Ibid., 43.

CHAPTER THIRTEEN
"THROW YOURSELF INTO CHRIST'S ARMS"

1. André Combes, *The Spirituality of St. Therese: An Introduction* (New York: P. J. Kenedy and Sons, 1950), 148–50.

2. Gerald Vann, *The Pain of Christ and the Sorrow of God* (New York: Alba House, 1994), 53.

3. Alice von Hildebrand, *The Privilege of Being a Woman* (Ypsilanti, Michigan: Veritas Press of Ave Maria University, 2002), 56–57.

4. Flannery O'Connor, Letter to A., February 4, 1961, in *Collected Works* (New York: The Library of America, 1988), 1144.

5. Letter to A., September 15, 1955, in ibid., 956.

6. Elizabeth Fox-Genovese, "A Pro-Woman Pope: Why Radical Feminists Can't Hear the Good Words John Paul II Has for Women", *Christianity Today* 42, no. 5 (April 27, 1998): 73–75.

CHAPTER FOURTEEN
LONGING FOR FLANNERY

1. Flannery O'Connor, Letter to Louise Abbot, n.d., in *Collected Works* (New York: The Library of America, 1988), 1110.

2. Joanne Mosely, *Edith Stein: Modern Saint and Martyr* (Mahwah, New Jersey: Hidden Spring, 2006), 44.

3. Flannery O'Connor, Letter to A., August 2, 1955, in *Collected Works*, 943.

4. Letter to Carl Hartman, March 2, 1954, in ibid., 922.

5. Ibid., 919.

6. Letter to A., November 25, 1960, in ibid., 1137.

EPILOGUE
"EVERYTHING IS A GRACE"

1. Thérèse of Lisieux, *Prayers and Meditations of Thérèse of Lisieux*, ed. Cindy Cavnar (Ann Arbor, Michigan: Servant Publications, 1991), 167.

2. Thomas Merton, *The Living Bread* (New York: Dell Publishing Company, 1959), 36.

3. Gerald Vann, *The Pain of Christ and the Sorrow of God* (New York: Alba House, 1994), 79.

4. Ibid., 80.

5. Flannery O'Connor, Letter to Alfred Corn, May 30, 1962, in *Collected Works* (New York: The Library of America, 1988), 1164.

6. Thérèse of Lisieux, *St. Thérèse of Lisieux: Her Last Conversations*, trans. John Clarke (Washington, D.C.: ICS Publications, 1977), 57.

BIBLIOGRAPHY

Chesterton, G. K. *The Innocence of Father Brown*. London: Cassell and Company, 1911.

Combes, André. *The Spirituality of St. Thérèse: An Introduction*. Translated by Philip E. Hallett. New York: P. J. Kenedy and Sons, 1950.

————. "A Pro-Woman Pope: Why Radical Feminists Can't Hear the Good Words John Paul II Has for Women". *Christianity Today* 42, no 5 (April 27, 1998): 73–75.

Fox-Genovese, Elizabeth. *"Feminism Is Not the Story of My Life": How Today's Feminist Elite Has Lost Touch with the Real Concerns of Women*. New York: Nan A. Talese, 1996.

Hildebrand, Alice von. *The Privilege of Being a Woman*. Ypsilanti, Michigan: Veritas Press of Ave Maria College, 2002.

Hopkins, Gerard Manley. *The Poems of Gerard Manley Hopkins*. Edited by W. H. Gardner and N. H. MacKenzie. Oxford: Oxford University Press, 1970.

Lewis, C. S. *Mere Christianity*. New York: Macmillan, 1943, 1952.

————. *Surprised by Joy*. San Diego: Harcourt Brace and Company, 1955.

Merton, Thomas. *The Living Bread*. New York: Dell Publishing Company, 1956.

————. *The Seven Storey Mountain*. New York: Harcourt Brace Jovanovich, 1976.

Mosely, Joanne. *Edith Stein: Modern Saint and Martyr*. Mahwah, N.J.: Hidden Spring, 2006.

O'Connor, Flannery. *Flannery O'Connor: Collected Works*. New York: The Library of America, 1988.

Ratzinger, Cardinal Joseph. *God and the World: Believing and Living in Our Time—A Conversation with Peter Seewald*. Translated by Henry Taylor. San Francisco: Ignatius Press, 2002.

Thérèse of Lisieux. *Prayers and Meditations of Thérèse of Lisieux*. Edited by Cindy Cavnar. Ann Arbor, Michigan: Servant Publications, 1992.

————. *St. Therese of Lisieux: Her Last Conversations*. Translated by John Clarke. Washington, D.C.: ICS Publications, 1977.

Thomas a Kempis. *The Imitation of Christ*. New York: Catholic Book Publishing Company, 1993.

Thompson, Francis. *Selected Poems of Francis Thompson*. London: Methuen and Company, 1909.

Tolstoy, Leo. *Leo Tolstoy: Spiritual Writings*. Edited by Charles E. Moore. Maryknoll, N.Y.: Orbis Books, 2006.

Vann, Gerald. *The Pain of Christ and the Sorrow of God*. New York: Alba House, 1994.